CONTENTS

Joe Sutherland Gould, the head of his own
public relations agency, is the author of
*How to Publicize Yourself, Your Family, and
Your Organization* (Prentice-Hall/Spectrum
Books, 1983).

Prentice-Hall International, Inc., *London*
Prentice-Hall of Australia Pty. Limited, *Sydney*
Prentice-Hall Canada Inc., *Toronto*
Prentice-Hall of India Private Limited, *New Delhi*
Prentice-Hall of Japan, Inc., *Tokyo*
Prentice-Hall of Southeast Asia Pte. Ltd., *Singapore*
Whitehall Books Limited, *Wellington, New Zealand*
Editora Prentice-Hall do Brasil Ltda., *Rio de Janeiro*

Joe Sutherland Gould

DON'T THROW IT OUT— SELL IT

CONVERT THE CLUTTER IN YOUR CLOSETS INTO CASH IN YOUR POCKETS

A SPECTRUM BOOK

Prentice-Hall, Inc., Englewood Cliffs, New Jersey 07632

4-3-89

Library of Congress Cataloging in Publication Data

Gould, J. Sutherland.
    Don't throw it out—sell it.

    "A Spectrum Book"
    Includes index.
    1. Secondhand trade—Handbooks, manuals, etc.
I. Title.
HF5482.G68   1983   658.8'7   83-9468
ISBN 0-13-218487-7
ISBN 0-13-218479-6 (pbk.)

For Nancy and Jodie

10 9 8 7 6 5 4 3 2 1

ISBN 0-13-218487-7

ISBN 0-13-218479-6 {PBK.}

Photos by Anne Brown

Editorial/production supervision by Chris McMorrow
Cover design by Hal Siegel
Manufacturing buyer: Doreen Cavallo

This book is available at a special discount when ordered in
bulk quantities. Contact Prentice-Hall, Inc., General
Publishing Division, Special Sales, Englewood Cliffs, N.J. 07632.

CONVERTING CLOSET CLUTTER INTO CASH

1

Today the clutter in your closet or basement, once considered junk, can be converted into cash. One of the biggest business booms in the United States producing substantial profits for amateur merchants is the garage sale. Weekend entrepreneurs in every part of the country are earning money by selling their castoffs not only from garages but in yards, basements, driveways, barns and from porches, homes, and apartments. A sale can net from $100 to $400. When people team with neighbors or hold multifamily sales, the receipts usually amount to well over $1,000.

Why are increasing numbers of people selling items they once considered junk? Most saleholders queried said it was a relatively easy way to make extra cash at a time when inflation is shredding their pocketbooks. And more people recognize that the garage sale, the old consumer practice of buying and selling second-hand goods, has regained respectability.

A widow living in New York City said, "I felt it was very undignified to sell things I wanted to throw out. But being pressed for money, I participated in a block sale my neighbors held. The pleasure and enthusiasm people showed when they found something they liked made the whole thing a delightful experience."

With the prices of new products distressingly high as a result of inflation, people are finding it wise to compromise, particularly when it means considerable savings. When a man bought an old but still working toaster for two dollars at a suburban garage sale outside of Philadelphia, he commented, "It will do just as well as a new one that would cost me ten times the price."

An elderly lady in Houston not only finds that merchandise is priced attractively at the sales she attends but also noted that "so many new things you buy today just fall apart." Garage sales are a bonanza for newlyweds coping with tight budgets. With patience, they can find a bounty of fine home furnishings at a fraction of their original cost. Many of the pieces are elegant enough to grace the homes of the affluent. At many sales, shoppers will find new merchandise such as Christmas, anniversary, and wedding gifts offered at drastic discounts.

In addition to the cost-conscious buyers who make up most of the estimated millions of people who attend these cash and carry sell-a-thons every weekend, there is the Cadillac crowd looking for a fabulous find. They are out to discover a painting worth thousands being sold by an unwary saleholder for a handful of dollars, or an antique tossed into the pile of low-price discards that is truly a treasure.

The garage sale is not just a casual outing for the merchants who make their livelihoods from selling second-hand products. Unlike the amateur bargain sleuth, professional dealers are truly experts at distinguishing bric-a-brac from quality pieces being sold at giveaway prices. Antique dealers often pick up their most profitable wares at these sales. Therefore, if you suspect that anything you have might be extremely valuable, take it to an appraiser. It will be worth the fee to be assured that you are not about to sell a priceless possession at a regrettably low figure.

Everything at a tag sale is saleable—literally. The variety of items displayed and bought is truly astounding. You should never be the least bit hesitant about putting up for sale all the junk you have accumulated. There is really a buyer for everything at a garage sale.

Along with your old appliances, furniture, clocks, radios, dishes, and silverware, put out those half empty bottles of perfume, whatever is left in used paint cans, machinery parts, battered typewriters, musty wigs, worn tires, and even empty beer cans and mayonnaise jars. There is a collector for nearly everything and always someone looking for hard-to-find parts that are out of production. People who have conducted these sales say, "You just would not believe the stuff people will buy." One man said he sold a box of tattered towels. It was bought by a service station owner who needed rags.

A shy lady anxious to earn extra money finally overcame her embarrassment and arranged her first garage sale. Being a reluctant weekend merchant, she displayed only selected items from her collection of clutter. Selling everything within four hours, she was encouraged to hold another sale but this time without any self-imposed restrictions. The lady from Atlanta admitted, "The second time I put out things that I would have been ashamed for people to know I saved." She sold them, too.

The garage sale proliferation across the country has Americans learning more about competitive selling. Your sale will almost never be the only one in the community. In some areas, there are up to 100 advertised every weekend. Buyers then know they can comparison shop very easily. Therefore, you will have to negotiate with shoppers who expect to pay less than the asking price. Good-natured bargaining generally ends in a successful transaction. And it is fun, too.

In fact, there is a friendly, often party-like atmosphere at these home merchandising marts. People of all ages attend, browse, and amuse themselves with random observations about the items being sold. At times, families will rest long enough to refresh themselves with hot chocolate or iced tea from their thermos jugs. Many new friendships are made, and holding a sale is one way to get to know your neighbors better, especially those who live down the block or up the road.

Do you know of anything that is tax-free today? Well, you do now. Despite the gargantuan reach of the Internal Revenue Service, it hasn't yet touched the area of home sales. The official attitude is that the profits people make are trifling compared to the original cost of the merchandise. Of course, if you decide to hold a sale every week, the IRS might show some interest in your cottage enterprise.

Sales tax collectors also ignore garage sales. The comment of a spokesman for the Texas comptroller of public accounts seems to reflect the prevailing point of view nationally. He said it was impractical and a waste of taxpayers' money to monitor them. True, indeed. In sprawling Westchester County just next to New York City, there are over 200 yard, home, moving, and joint-family sales held every weekend. Many states, like Georgia, categorize these sales as casual transactions of merchandise and do not tax them.

How far has the garage sale come in the last decade? It has developed into something more than just a homestyle selling venture. Several years ago, Evanston, Illinois, sponsored the "Largest Garage Sale in the World." It was like a flea market where space was rented to participants. Booths set up on the five floors of the city's parking garage cost a resident a rental fee of $7.50. With this ready-made display space arranged in a convenient location in the heart of the city, a sales enthusiast could easily make a sizeable profit by selling just a few junk items.

Before holding a garage sale, it is advisable to find out if any local civic ordinances covering such an event exist. Although most places are still free of any restrictions, many towns are now setting guidelines for such sales and require permits. Homeowners in Dearborn, Michigan, must pay a token fee for holding the first sale, a higher one for the second, and an increased set amount for each succeeding one. Orange County, Florida, permits families to hold only one sale every six months.

Sale controls were introduced by many cities and communities following the complaints of neighbors about inconsiderate shoppers who park on lawns and block driveways with their cars, and saleholders who post signs indiscriminately.

When should you use a professional tag sale organizer? When selling the entire contents of a home or apartment because of moving, relocation, or divorce. A sale of this size will be far more lucrative when a tag sale expert is used to establish the proper market value of merchandise, identify antiques, and sell them at the right prices. The home contents sale organization also knows where and how to advertise, has a private mailing list of past customers who are sent postcard invitations, knows how to maintain crowd control when people swarm through your home, and skillfully sets up needed security measures.

For these expert services, which will almost always yield a higher cash return than an ambitious do-it-yourself effort, the tag sale professional gets a commission of approximately 20 to 25 percent.

For the future, remember that castoffs are worth money, so don't throw anything out—sell it.

PLANNING YOUR SALE

Now that you have decided to cash in on your clutter, how do you start? First, by committing yourself to an act of separation. Overcome any reluctance you have to pick and choose what you will sell. Get rid of everything that has been stored in basements and attics. Get rid of that collection of forgotten items put away for tomorrow. Tomorrow never comes for most people.

This hesitation to part with castoffs is a national affliction that can be called "discard ambivalence." It is an ailment that is due to viral uncertainty. It produces a twilight thinking such as "I might use that coat again," or "I'll hold that broiler for one of the kids."

Usually neither ever happens. Later, upon reinspection, the coat provokes grimaces and sighs that mean, "Why did I ever save that thing?" Keeping appliances for your kids, especially if they are just 8 and 12 years old, is another folly. By the time the kids are old enough to use them, the kitchen unit will be a replica of rust ready to crumble at first touch. Then there is the parental disappointment when older children, ready to go on their own, reject these pass-ons. Try money; *that* never gets shrugged off.

One test to allow you to decide clearly if you are ready to part with a collectible is to ask yourself, "Have I really ever retrieved anything from that pile of Don't Fits, Out-of-Dates, and Tired-of-Wearing clothes or from that shelf of 'I don't need or use that any more' appliances?"

The remedy for discard ambivalence is: Everything you don't use or need goes. To motivate yourself to accept this sweeping state of mind, use the B.F. Skinner technique. Reward yourself for such dramatic action. Think of something you want to buy with the profits made from your outdoor sale. Enjoy the image of a pleasing new purchase.

Emptying the house of clutter and freeing your closets from sartorial congestion (can't squeeze another thing in here) is an accomplishment of significant satisfaction.

SEARCH AND FIND

You have unrealized profit in every room of the house. Remember, what you see is really not all you have to sell. In addition to the basement, garage, and crawlspace, there is sale treasure to be found everywhere.

Organize a methodical search-and-find mission that will have you looking into every closet, drawer, and idle box in your home. Think of the bounty that is in your kitchen—from unused pots and dishes to small appliances hidden and forgotten in remote closet corners, under your counters, and beneath the sink.

Of course, don't forget the kids' rooms, the den, and the bathrooms. Like to update that old scale? Sell the one you have now and then buy a new one.

Do not be casual about this odyssey of discovery. You have nothing to gain but money and the delight of getting rid of your personal junk. Therefore, don't just peek into your closets, take everything out. Be sure you inspect every corner, especially those out-of-sight, out-of-mind hideaways. Be ready for some surprises. More than once you will probably shriek, "So that's where it is." And even more often you'll say, "Why am I saving that?"

When you are about to shift back into the hesitation hop, give yourself a simple truth quiz.

Do I really want that?
Am I likely to ever use it again?
Am I tired of that?
Is it really worth saving for my kids?

Most parents have found that clinging to possible pass-ons becomes a matter of saving what will be thrown out later.

Often personal items are uncovered that were sought after for years but never found. One man found his World War II sergeant's uniform. Trying it on, he discovered that, although one arm managed to slide through the sleeve, the jacket did not reach his other shoulder. However, it did look good draped over a wooden hanger, decorated with battle ribbons. Committed to a total clean out, he abandoned sentiment and sold it at his garage sale for a tidy sum.

What do you have in the attic? Boxes and bows and worn out clothes and other things stored away too long ago to remember. Even once cherished keepsakes barely stir faded memories. You might wonder why you ever considered keeping many of them. Browse through this garage sale bounty and avoid becoming a victim of the eternal postponement syndrome. Delay no longer.

Try to put as few things as possible in your new file-for-future pile. The next time you review these items you put on hold, you will very likely wonder why the decision to sell was so hard to make the first time through. As you know, more things are kept for sentimental uncertainty than are ever warranted. Truly precious mementos of your past that perk the memory are generally visible around the house or secure in places where they are accessible.

TO CLEAN OR NOT TO CLEAN

Keep in mind that slightly soiled and aging merchandise have the bargain look. Backyard shoppers expect these wares to have a worn and weathered appearance. Garage sale seekers are prepared to brighten and polish their purchases at home. In fact, these shoppers take personal pleasure in restoring their bargain buys to the nearly new look. So hold off the muscle power and do not scrub your pieces to glitter like merchandise on the shelves of local merchants.

Sonny and Carol Kiley of Katonah, New York, who are professionals at conducting garage sales for people, advise keeping a small amount of respectable dirt on most things. However, they clearly caution against displaying anything that is out-right dirty. The subtle distinction that creates the impression that an item has been used, but not that much, is ideal. "You are catering to a bargain mentality," explains Carol.

Some of your customers will be veterans of many sales. But don't be intimidated by these careful buyers. Even they get stuck once in a while. Carol remembers that at one sale, a middle-aged man, who was inspecting merchandise with great expertise, studied a music box that was on display. The inner struggle to decide whether this was a buy or not prevailed for quite a while. Shaking his head in a gesture of uncertainty, he put it down and declared he would come back the next day. (Normally this is an unwise decision because low-priced items sell quickly.)

Returning the following day, the man grinned at his good fortune. Still available for sale was the slightly tarnished but handsome music box. He examined it again and convinced himself that he was about to score a consumer coup.

After the man quibbled over the ten dollar price tag with the skill of a practiced negotiator, Carol dropped the price to $8.50, exactly what she expected to make for the item. She then rejected the man's counter-offer to buy the music box for seven dollars. While paying the $8.50, the happy shopper seemed to be beaming triumphantly. According to Carol's professional appraisal, she knew the man thought he had captured an antique trophy that had escaped the notice of the garage sale pros.

Reaching to take the box to bag it, Carol saw the man's ruddy pallor melt into somber ashen gray. "My God," moaned the man, devastated by discovering the original price tag under the box, "It cost only five dollars new."

"Well," shrugged Carol, "what can I tell you. That's inflation."

Failing to remove the original price tag was an error, admitted Carol. Asked if this is some kind of personal vengeance she takes out on garage sale addicts who come with an almost maniacal determination to find an underpriced gem, she grinned and said, "Maybe that's why I overlooked it. But it *was* an oversight. What amused me is that this man was so excited by what he thought was a special discovery that he never examined the music box thoroughly. He became careless."

BEST SALE DAYS

Saturday and Sunday are the most popular garage sale days but not always the best ones, according to Letitia Willie, a garage sale expert who now counsels people on how to make their sales more successful. Letitia, a graduate of the New York Institute of Fashion who spent several years working at the bridal registry of B. Altman's Department Store in New York City, prefers Friday and Saturday sale days.

"Sunday is for lookers," observes Letitia. "People out

for a drive stop by to browse just to have something to do. Sure some sales are made, but not enough to make up for personal wear and tear."

Why is Friday better? Letitia explains that more women are free to come on that day without their kids. She added, "These are serious buyers not just looking for bargains but to purchase things they need for their home and children.

What are the best days for you? Simply the ones that you find most convenient. But keep in mind that when other pros were asked about Friday being an especially good sale day, they agreed. However, it was pointed out that to prepare for a Friday meant getting everything ready by Thursday night. Having to devote two weekdays to a home sale is more than most people can manage.

WHAT'S IN A NAME?

A garage sale called by any other name is just the same. Some enterprising, pioneer do-it-yourselfer probably started it all by selling his discards in a barn. For years after, this type of home engineered selling was called the "barn sale" and was conducted largely in rural areas.

However, when people migrated to the suburbs after World War II, many apartment dwellers suddenly became home-owners with large, inviting areas to store trash. "Don't throw it out—keep it, we have plenty of room," became a national indulgence. When Junior's old toys and Dad's wayward home purchases (Gee, I guess I can use this one day) crowded every available space, it was time to get rid of this personal junk. Lingering memories of the barn sale inspired some suburbanites to experiment with selling their old stuff to neighbors by displaying the merchandise in their garages. It was the most convenient place. And with the passion that existed for manicured lawns and neighborhood orderliness, who would be brazen enough to cart out the attic trash and sell it in front of the house? No one, at least not in the very early periods of suburban growth.

When garages became too cramped, backyards beckoned. This location was out of neighbors' view and allowed much more attic and closet treasure to be shown to the public. Profits were all the motivation needed to expand the garage sale to any suitable outdoor area where more buyers could be accommodated.

For a while "garage sale" was used as the generic name for selling used merchandise anywhere around the home, but sales today are called by titles that designate why they are being held, or where the used merchandise came from.

Yard Sale
Driveway Sale
Moving Sale
Retirement Sale
Multifamily Sale
Block Sale
Apartment Sale
Home Contents Sale
Divorce Sale
Tag Sale
Attic Sale

FUN AND PROFIT

People who hold sales usually enjoy the experience as much as the profits. They find bargaining, except with an occasional obnoxious shopper, to be exciting. The extra dollar or two for an item frequently is less important than the price victory over an opponent. Many people find this is the first time they have engaged their neighbors down the street in any lengthy conversation. New friendships are made. And seeing years of clutter disappear is the prize pleasure of them all.

WHAT TO SELL

Almost everything can be sold at your sale. Therefore, don't throw anything out—sell it. People who have held garage sales keep confirming repeatedly that "your trash is someone else's treasure."

This is true even if you have a pile of oddities that can qualify as junk. You might have fragments and pieces of machinery, broken clocks, radios, half-filled cans of paint, nearly empty bottles of lotion or aftershave, and other items that no longer function. There are the bottle people who will pay 10 or 15 cents for your containers and others who need just half a can of paint for a small job.

THE SEARCH FOR PARTS

There is a tenacious core of consumers that use products until they almost literally disintegrate. These are the people always looking for parts for products no longer being made. Garage sales have proven to be one of the best sources for replacement needs. It is amazing to learn what people are looking for: a gear for an antiquated motor, a main spring for a mantle clock, knobs for old radios manufactured when Rudy Vallee crooned to a swooning American audience.

There are also the television parts seekers looking for tubes and other components for sets made just after World War II. Some are still maintaining the very first sets sold before the war.

Almost nothing ends up as absolute junk, even those bits and pieces you thought were certified candidates for the garbage collector. At a garage sale, they will bring you extra dollars.

SOME BIG SELLERS

The garage sale pros agree that furniture is one of the hottest sale items in the country. While the continual upward swing in the cost of living has forced more people to budget cautiously, the high price of new furniture has driven consumers to find what they need at backyard sales.

Check the cost of brand new living, dining, and bedroom furniture; check the prices being asked for kitchen chairs and tables that appear as sturdy as match sticks. Staggering! It's not only the cost that has created buyer resistance but also the tasteless designs and questionable craftsmanship of today's products.

Swarms of shoppers look for their household furnishings at garage sales, hoping to find pieces made 20 or more years ago when style and patient workmanship were expected of new products.

Not all the furniture seekers are people forced to shop the second-hand market because of economic pressures. There are nearly as many consumers who can afford the high price tags found on the glistening new pieces displayed in showrooms.

These buyers have a reverence for quality and will not compromise with the shoddy values offered today. Therefore, the pursuit for fine old furniture has been expanded to include the people who want something better for their money.

Many newlyweds have no option. They are forced into the garage sale hunt. They know that they can eventually find enough good furniture to fill every room of their apartment or house for a few hundred dollars. Often the price of just one new large piece of furniture will cost more. Seen in large numbers at garage sales, they simply explain that it is the most practical way—and for many young married couples, the *only* way—to furnish their first living quarters.

Furniture shoppers look for pieces that have been well-made. Many will buy furniture that is tattered and gutted if it has an artistic shape and if the frame is made of solid wood that has not deteriorated. Oak is extremely popular and sells fast. Knowing that a fine old piece can be restored and still cost much less than a poorly manufactured new one has heightened the demand for old furniture.

Now there is no need to be embarrassed by putting out your worn, dirty old couch. You could get up to $40 for it. For very special pieces, even more. A buyer of a piece of furniture that is more dirty than battered can have a new-looking piece for the living room by putting on slip covers.

OTHER GOOD SELLERS

Most men will go directly to your display of garden equipment and tools, which should be in reasonably good working order. Saws, hammers, ladders, screwdrivers of every type, and even nails will sell.

Appliances move well, too. There will be a buyer for anything that is still functioning—lamps, television sets, washing machines, dryers, coffee makers, dishwashers (a luxury product many people would never buy new but will acquire when the price is right), radios, stereo components, clocks, pots, and china.

Don't hesitate to put out towels, linens, bathroom shower curtains, tablecloths, and cloth napkins, especially if an entire set is available. These items move.

Do kids ever have enough toys or games? Generally more than enough, but parents don't think so. They will devour your old toys. Books will sell and boxes full of bric-a-brac will also earn extra dollars for you.

"There is a whole new market of buyers looking for children's things," noted Jill Goldstone, owner of the Garage Sales Store in Pleasantville, New York. "We just can't keep up with the demand for such items as cribs, basinettes, strollers, playpens, and carriages," said Jill.

"It is not so much the parents who are searching for these baby things, but grandparents," she explained. "What has happened," she continued, "is that Grandma and Grandpa, hoping to have their children visit more often, buy items that cannot be easily transported from one house to the other. Having a playpen, carriage, and highchair on hand makes visiting the grandfolks so much easier. In fact, it permits the children to stay over for a night or two—something I found that grandparents want to encourage."

Jill noted that when a shipment of baby items arrives at her store on Friday, it is completely sold out by Saturday afternoon to what she calls the "second market."

CLOTHES—UNCERTAIN SELLERS

One professional garage sale coordinator observed that the sale of clothes depends largely on the economic status of a community. In the more affluent areas, the sale of old clothes lags, despite the condition of the garments. Letitia Willie had a new navy blue wool coat worth $200 for sale. Inspected but passed over by shoppers during her two-day, outdoor sell-a-thon, she was finally offered ten dollars by a woman who intimated she was doing Letitia a favor by taking it off her hands. Declining the bid, the wool coat was taken to another area where the income level was considerably lower and sold to a thrift shop for $40.

Designer clothes in good condition have a slightly better chance of being purchased in high income locations than in middle-class areas, but they will sell even better in blue collar neighborhoods. Still, as some expects point out, they may not move quickly.

During the three years Jill Goldstone has operated her garage sale shop, she has been so discouraged with the demand for clothes that she does not carry any garments in her store. "They just hang around too long while other merchandise moves quickly," Jill said.

Even less in demand are manual typewriters. Unless the machine is a genuine antique, it will not sell easily. That quaint old Remington noiseless long ago phased out of production could fetch ten dollars by someone who might like to use it as a display piece.

Mattresses do not attract much attention and, for that matter, not too many buyers. This is a particularly personal piece of merchandise that most shoppers veer away from. Many people tend to enshrine this sleep-piece with all sorts of gloom and terrifying fictional tales, so that second-hand mattresses almost become fearful objects. Demand may be low also because people rarely replace their mattresses; they become so attached to them that they use them interminably.

While many old magazines sell for as much as 50¢ and a few have become certified collectibles, those *National Geographics* you have carefully stored in your basement are among the least saleable publications. Yes, they will go for about 10 or 15 cents but hardly command the blockbuster prices people anticipate.

SOUGHT-AFTER MISSING PARTS

Here is a list of items that most likely will move quickly.

Pot tops
Refrigerator baskets
Refrigerator shelves
Various size bowls for Mixmasters
China, glasses, and plates to replace ones missing from sets

WHAT'S NEW HERE?

You might be asked this question several times during the course of a sale. Why? Most likely you will have some brand new merchandise at your outdoor market. It could be Christmas, anniversary, or mother's and father's day gifts that failed to please. You looked at them once, then you put them away forever. Some other presents might have been used once or twice but are still practically new.

Like everyone else, you probably bought some product in a flush of enthusiasm only to find that you soon tired of it or really did not like it at all. No doubt there were other enticing purchases you made only to abandon them to your scrap heap in short order. This is particularly true of clothes. That shirt, blouse, suit, or dress you thought looked so smart on you in the store, you decided was a disaster when you took it home. Now they hang like mocking space thieves in your congested closets. These should be put on the selling block.

What's new at your sale? A lot more than you thought at first. An electric weed cutter was offered at a sale for ten dollars. Used only three times, the owner found trimming hard to reach grass, a tiny patch at a time, a tedious process and was annoyed by the long electrical cord he had to continually move from place to place. When a customer said he would take it for five dollars, it was sold. Later the man admitted it became part of his own clutter. "I put it in my garage, planning to buy the cutting string that was missing, and forgot all about it."

But will people really buy almost anything? Yes. They will even bid for your cigarette lighter if you absent-mindedly put it down on the display table. At home sales, shoppers will forage through closets and make offers on canned goods and boxes of spaghetti.

The most unusual request the Kileys had was for something that was not for sale. It came from a man they found looking at mail taken from a desk. Not only was the room clearly designated as not for shoppers, but the doors were locked. The invasion into the personal property of the home-owners for whom the Kileys were conducting the sale was outrageous.

"True," declared Sonny Kiley. "During the 12 years we have been conducting professional garage and home content sales, we have come across some very weird behavior in people. We expect almost anything at any time."

Did this man qualify for the Guinness book of surprises? "He might have, if there was such a book," Sonny Kiley assured me. "The man was middle-aged and rather scholarly looking," Sonny recalled. "After I told him firmly that he broke into this room that was shut to shoppers, he was polite and apologetic. When I wanted to take the letters from him, he pulled them back and asked me if he could just remove the stamps."

For the next several hours, he sat at the desk and cautiously removed the stamps, carefully avoiding damaging the letters.

GETTING RID OF LEFTOVERS

While everything will eventually sell, not everything is sold at one sale. You can keep the remainders for your next mercantile venture or sell it all to a thrift shop.

Most of these stores, which stock second-hand goods, will buy out your sale failures without inspecting every item you have. The proprietors risk that enough saleable merchandise will be found among your remainders to make the total purchase profitable. You will be given only a fraction of what you could earn at your own sale, but it is the simplest way to get rid of all the things that did not sell and that you really no longer want to keep around.

If you would like to donate your leftovers, you will find that hospitals and local charitable organizations might take what you have for their fund-raising thrift sale days. They do not always take everything. In fact, even the Salvation Army is now selective in what it will remove from your premises.

ANTIQUES
OR JUST
ANCIENT

"My goodness," whispered the lady who was holding her first yard sale, "that man bought this broken, old tin toy." Her daughter smiled back and said, "You know what they say. There is a customer for everything at these sales. I believe it now."

The man, walking to his car unaware of the chuckles behind him, had discovered a treasure among the trash.

Mitchell Goldstone, president of a New York conglomerate, is a weekend aid to his wife Jill at the Garage Sale Store. During the three years the store has been open, Mitch and Jill have developed an uncanny scavenger instinct for finding valuable pieces among the discards at garage sales.

At one time, the slight, thin-haired executive would also have scoffed at the toy he bought and thought, "Why the heck would anyone want this battered piece of tin?" Experience has given him the wisdom to know what to look for in the junk piles. Having bought out the remains of an estate sale one time, he found a broken sand toy at the bottom of a bag filled with bric-a-brac. Uncertain about the value of the item, his first impulse was to throw it out. But after studying it for a while, he decided to test his indecisiveness.

Mitch had the toy mended and placed without price on the desk in the Garage Sale Store. To the average shopper, the piece was ornamental and obviously not for sale. However, to sharp-eyed dealers that prowl through garage sales to find a treasure casually displayed by an unwary homeowner, the toy was a prize purchase.

One dealer glanced casually at the piece and with a hint of disdain told Goldstone he would give him five dollars for it. The offer was refused as Mitch had decided he would sell it for $10. The small sand toy, with its buckets still ready to function for the pleasure of some tot, remained on the desk.

The next offer came from a dealer who was less able to mask his interest. "Say," he puffed out in asthmatic appreciation, "I'll give you $25 just to take that off your hands." The jump from a bid of $5 to $25 keyed Goldstone to the fact that he might have a valuable item.

An emerging dealer himself, Goldstone decided to keep the attractive tin toy out for future antique hunters to see. Four weeks later a dealer friend dropped in to look at new acquisitions at the Garage Sale Store and declared flatly, "I'll give you $250 for that toy."

"Sold," snapped the stunned Goldstone.

The dealer then turned to Goldstone and grinned, "I'll get $500 for this." He explained, "It's an 1890 German sand toy, and it still has some original paint on it."

You must be cautious when you inspect garage sale items in your basement and attic. Not every old thing you have will qualify as an antique. Still, if you have any doubts about the value of the piece you plan to sell, get it appraised. In fact, set aside everything you believe is worth evaluation and have a professional tell you if they are antiques or collectibles.

GETTING ITEMS APPRAISED

Can you get a truly accurate appraisal? Most of the garage sale pros interviewed seemed very skeptical about ever getting a real-value evaluation of merchandise, due to the way appraisers are compensated. Judy Sclier, a partner in Tag-Along Girls, an organization of four women who conduct home contents and apartment sales, explained, "Since appraisers get a percentage of the total amount of the merchandise's estimated value, they will appraise high. Some of our clients become very upset when we give them the realistic price they can expect to get compared to the fantasy figures they were given."

What is the best way to find a conscientious appraiser? Make inquiries. Good recommendations come from friends who have had satisfactory experiences with their appraisers. This simply means that these people had their valuables appraised at prices that matched the current buying in the marketplace.

If your friends cannot yield any hopeful prospects, you can get the names of professional appraisers in your area who specialize in various wares by writing to the American Society of Appraisers, International Headquarters, P.O. Box 17265, Washington, D.C., 20041. The organization states that it is "America's only nationwide, multidisciplinary appraisal testing and designation society."

A.S.A. has over 5,000 members who operate in 80 chapters in the United States and abroad. Among the participants, whom the Society notes are tested and certified, are specialists in antiques, fine arts, gems, jewelry, and every type of item that can be considered potentially extremely valuable.

The Society's annual publication "Professional Appraisers Services Directory," costs eight dollars. Other pamphlets available for just a self-addressed, stamped envelope are "Directory of Certified Professional Personal Property Appraisers," "Information on the Appraisal Profession," and "The Public and Appraisers Pro Bono Publico."

OTHER SUGGESTIONS

Here are some tips on getting many of your precious items appraised without paying for the service. Paintings and jewelry will still need the crafty eye of the experts, but nearly everything else can be evaluated by working professionals.

1. Call several dealers and have them bid on your special household treasures. Keep in mind that these people will be giving you evaluations that will be about one-third of the true value of your merchandise. Remember, they are retail merchants eager to snare bargains. After at least three dealers have priced your saleables, determine the probable market price sold from your home and not from a shop. Consumers always expect to pay more at a shop. Remember that the dealer will have restored the piece to some extent to make it more attractive to customers. Remember, too, that the dealer can wait to sell, slowly reducing the price over a period of time. Since you want to move your discards (even the valuable ones) within the limits of a two or three day sale, tag your specials to appeal to the bargain brigades that will storm your property.

2. Experienced thrift and consignment shop proprietors are savvy buyers. Call in a Jill Goldstone for a price look. Since these are community type folk who are not the huckstering hawks that dealers are, you will get a fair appraisal. These business people are interested in securing your leftovers and establishing reputations as honorable merchants in the area.

3. Visit a flea market and invite some of the vendors selling antique items to your home to inspect what you have for sale. You will get a good line on value from the prices they offer.

4. Professionals who conduct home contents sales, apartment, and garage sales for people are always interested in acquiring special pieces that they could add to one of their sales. They will make offers on your potential antiques and col-

lectibles. While these pros will usually offer more than a dealer, still you can consider it as about one-half the market value, or less. Again, you must adjust the price for a home sale. If you live in a more affluent area, you can take the liberty of opting for a higher mark-up.

5. If you still feel you have a priceless item after all of the gratuitous evaluation, then get to the library and do a little research. You will probably get the best indication of what an item is worth with this kind of effort. You also will be better informed about pricing in the future and more alert as to what items not to regard lightly at your garage sale.

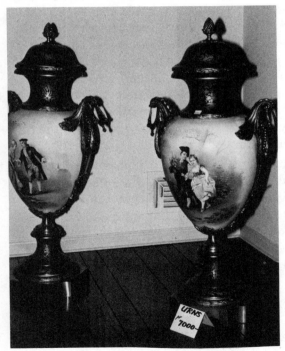

FIGURE 1. A pair of Sezeres, late 19th century, 37-inch-high urns, genuine antiques, sold for slightly under the asking price of $7,000.

FIGURE 2. Earthenware containers and a vase that hint at being antiques are only modest-price merchandise.

HELPFUL PUBLICATIONS

Trade magazines are among the best sources of objective information on trends and prices. These publications are written expressly for professionals and for people who are active or extremely interested in a special field. There are several published in the United States that cover antiques and collectibles. If you plan to maintain a continuing involvement with valuables, you might like to consider subscribing to a magazine whose editorial thrust is most suitable to your particular interests. The best way to determine what publication you might need is to buy one copy before subscribing.

If you are looking merely for information about a particular subject, then write to the magazine and inquire whether any article has been written on the antique or collectible you are planning to sell. If such a piece was published, order that issue. Always eager to expand their circulation, you will find the circulation departments of these special publications most accommodating.

Here are some trade publications devoted to antiques and collectibles:

Antiques and Arts Weekly
Newtown, CT 06470
News of antiques and lists of flea market locations

Antiques & Collectibles
P.O. Box 22186
Lexington, KY 40522
Current information on both subjects

Antique Monthly
2015 Sixth Street
Tuscaloosa, AL 35401
Market trends and reports, question and answer columns

Antiques Journal
100 Bryant
P.O. Box 1046
Dubuque, IA 52001

Authorative articles on all phases of antiques and collectibles

Antiques Magazine
551 Fifth Avenue
New York, NY 10017

American and European antiques, primarily from the seventeenth to nineteenth centuries

Antiques Price Report
P.O. Box 974
Kermit, TX 79745

Each issue covers a different area of collecting

The Antiques Dealer
1115 Clifton Avenue
P.O. Box 2147
Clifton, NJ 07013

Information about price trends

Joel Sater's Antiques News
P.O. Box B
Marietta, PA 17557

News and features about antiques, collectibles, auctions, antique shows, fleamarkets, with emphasis on Eastern states

The Plate Collector
P.O. Box 1041
Kermit, TX 79745

Price trends on current collectible plates

Relics
1012 Edgecliff Terrace
Box 3338
Austin, TX 78764

Articles on antiques and miscellaneous collectibles

Antique Trader Weekly
P.O. Box 1050
Dubuque, IA 52001

In depth articles on antiques and items that qualify as collectibles.

Antique Automobile
501 W. Governor Road
P.O. Box 417
Hershey, PA 17033

Office publication of the Antique Automobile Club of America

Antique Motor News
919 South Street
Long Beach, CA 90805

For people interested in collecting and restoring antique automobiles

COLLECTIBLES

The passionate wail for a collectible one year can become a dim whisper for the same item the next. Once collectors searched with zeal for beer cans as the nation's breweries shrunk from several hundred after the repeal of prohibition to a relative handful. Billy Beer, introduced hopefully as a profitable tribute to the flamboyant brother of former President Jimmy Carter, left only a legacy of hotly pursued beer cans. While ample collections of these containers can be found around the country, there is little demand for beer cans today.

Trends shift continually. Depression glass used mostly as incentives to motivate people to attend movies in the 1930s was one of the hot items a few years ago. As so much of it surfaced from the basements and attics of American homes, collectors began to ignore it as "too available."

Seasoned collectors appear to use this rule of thumb that directs their quest for collectibles: Mostly hard-to-find items that have some nostalgia are viewed as possible collectibles. Also, demand determines if an item makes it to this exalted status.

When buyers suddenly surface like a rash of measles dotted all over the national landscape, seeking and searching for a new piece, it's a collectible. One consideration always exists: Will the category of collectible contain enough variations to make up an interesting collection? At one time license plates were changed each year, providing an endless variety. Then, as an economic measure, most states stopped producing new vehicle plates and substituted an annual window sticker instead. The variety of old plates, and the fact that production was stopped, made license plates a popular collectible for a while—until it was discovered that they were too available.

Changing trends are beyond the control of the collector. On the other hand, commercial organizations will attempt to create a market of collectibles. Commemorative coins exploiting such national triumphs as the moon landing are sold to the public as future collector's items. Semiprecious stones have been suggested as investment collectibles certain to be worth more years later. Limited editions of prints and art have also been recommended as inflation hedges.

In the early 1970s many banks set up departments to advise clients about purchases that would ultimately be the most lucrative. Even these financial institutions bought art, expecting spectacular increases in its value within a few years. Many consumer publications began publishing the names of contemporary painters considered solid investments—like highly regarded securities. There appeared a chorus of assurance that everything would go up, up, and up.

People who speculated in commemorative coins found that when anything is sold in such massive numbers, it can take generations for those collectibles to have any appreciable value. Buyers of semiprecious stones found, for the most part, that they are even less precious years later.

The most disappointed speculators were those who believed that art, of almost any kind, can "only go up." Many unwisely bought highly promoted novelties that ultimately became as saleable as the stock of a bankrupt corporation. Even the more sophisticated buyers took losses instead of gains. The market value of an Andy Warhol has fallen to about half the original purchase price. Banks that bought art as "surefire" investments were embarrassed by the money they lost. Many of the pieces purchased, instead of escalating in price, became practically unmarketable.

The nation's mood about art changed drastically. Today there are few art collectors, although there are still some speculators.

CURRENT COLLECTIBLES

What are shoppers looking for most at this time? Items that are not necessarily dated but are in limited supply as the result of availability or because of controlled output originally. The extinct milk bottle is commanding a substantial price—an average of $100. Certain colored milk bottles are worth up to $4,000.

Here is a list of current "in-demand" collectibles:

Dolls
Items from the American occupation of Japan and from the U.S. zone in Germany
The first copy of Playboy (worth about $700)
Tin toys
Cast iron toys in good condition
Lone Ranger toys
Old photographs (if done by certain photographers)
Old postcards and match books
Beatle 45s in original record jackets (worth several hundred dollars)
Vintage rock or blues records in mint condition ($75; Caruso and Crosby records are not collectibles as too many were made)

Military uniforms or jackets
Celebrity memorabilia
Presidential memorabilia
Earhorn hearing aids
Corkscrews
Eye washing cups
Orange squeezers
Old stock certificates
Barbed wire (worth more if romantic history is available)
Comic books (old ones that originally cost five or ten cents)
Beer steins
Mugs
Guns
Swords
Selected match books (with unique ads; from historical night clubs or restaurants)
Baseball player cards
Political buttons
War posters
Medals
Boy Scout memorabilia
Camp Fire Girls items and publications
World's Fair memorabilia
Space Age memorabilia
Old Valentines
Unique Christmas decorations
Halloween toys and decorations
Unusual shot glasses
Nutcrackers
Sports memorabilia
Autographs
Original handwritten documents
Movie magazines published before 1940
Art deco

This list covers many items you might have in your home. Should you discover anything you believe might be characterized as a collectible, call several thrift shops for an opinion. They are listed in the telephone yellow pages under "Second-Hand Stores."

SELLING YOUR COLLECTIBLES

1. As you now know, to get the best price for your treasure you must sell it yourself. You can advertise in one of the trade publications listed in the previous chapters. You will be contacted by interested buyers who will request that you send a detailed description of your offering along with a color photograph or a photocopy if you have printed material about it. The sale can then be finalized by phone. Long distance calls are relatively inexpensive at night and during weekends. If you have a costly collectible to ship a long distance, talk with the person buying it. This is a good way to get some feeling about the buyer. Generally, people who are collectors are an honorable breed.

2. Take your collectible to a thrift shop where you can discuss leaving the collectible on consignment. The store will take 25 percent of the sale. Since the proprietor is obviously concerned about moving merchandise, the collectible will be marked down every 30 days. However, this is done only with your permission. Should an offer be made for the item that is less than the asking price, the shopowner will contact you for your approval before making the sale.

3. A convenient way to try and sell your treasure is to bring it to a neighbor's garage sale. If your item is accepted for the sale, you should pay your neighbor a commission of 10 or 15 percent. Be sure to establish a firm bottom price for the item as well as a tag (asking) price for shoppers to see and bargain down.

4. There is always the local newspaper or Pennysaver-type publication where you can advertise your collectible for direct sale.

5. If the piece is substantial and costly, it would be worth advertising it in the classified section of your major city paper. No matter where you live in relationship to the urban center, truly interested buyers will respond and consider it no problem to drive out and see the collectible.

6. Many people have succeeded in selling almost any kind of used merchandise by simply informing their neighbors through a simple flyer. It can be as simple as a typed up description of the item on your letterhead or plain white bond paper, together with a photocopy of the item.

7. If you have a genuine collectible and don't especially care how much you make selling it, contact a dealer. If a quick sale is your objective, you can conclude one rapidly.

Remember, if you find something around your house you believe might be a collectible, don't throw it out—*check* it out—and *then* sell it. The following is an important reference source:

The Encyclopedia of Collectibles
Time-Life Books
1271 Avenue of the Americas
New York, NY 10020

Many thrift shops have this special set of reference books available for the convenience of customers. Listed in this sixteen-set encyclopedia are all current collectibles from A to Z.

FIGURE 3. You can check the value of a collectible in *The Encyclopedia of Collectibles* published by Time-Life Books.

FIGURE 4. A sudden and growing demand for old and unique dolls has made this item an expensive collectible.

FIGURE 5. Buttons of the flap-eared, freckled face pup-
pet, "Howdy Doody," who charmed children on television in the 1950s, is an in-demand collectible.

44

FIGURE 6. Cast-iron toys are a more recent addition to the market of collectibles.

FIGURE 7. There is a steady and undiminished demand for railroad memorabilia. Postcards, buttons, trains sell well.

TYPE OF SALE
TO HOLD

As you have noticed, the area nearly always used for neighborhood merchandise marts is the driveway and lawn. It is a basic principle of marketing that visibility is essential to attracting customers. Merchandise displayed on tables in front of your home, with a large sign in front saying "Tag Sale," will attract passing motorists and pedestrians who will stop and make impulse purchases.

Of course, people coming to your sale because of your ads and posters will find your home easier when following your well-posted signs and then seeing your tables stacked with wares neatly arranged on your lawn.

Some people hesitate to hold a tag sale, commenting that they would feel terribly embarrassed by creating such a selling spectacle on their front lawns. Certainly the frequency with which this is being done today makes it an acceptable practice, as long as it does not become a common occurrence.

Still there are other homeowners who feel more comfortable holding the sale in their back yards. While their consideration for neighbors is noble, their location selection is most unfortunate, since product visibility is essential. That is why merchants spend so much time and money creating eye-catching window and in-store displays. They attract customers and move merchandise. With only a sign announcing a backyard sale, it would take the services of a carnival barker to persuade people to walk behind your house to inspect your castoffs.

APARTMENT SALE

City dwellers are more concerned today than ever about the prospect of bringing strangers into their apartments. Yet, the bonanza of buyers that one city block can yield is enough to guarantee a highly profitable sale. With the proper control, an apartment sale can be conducted safely.

One of the more comfortable ways to reach your consumer potential is to hold the sale just for the tenants of your apartment house. This also has some agreeable side benefits. You will get to know neighbors whom you have passed silently in the halls for years. These once anonymous faces will become real people and some will eventually become close friends. You may meet the neighbors whose loud stereos or rampaging kids thundering overhead you have tolerated without protest. Getting acquainted on your turf creates a friendly atmosphere for you to register a courteous complaint about these neighborly irritations. Instead of confrontation, you most likely will get cooperation.

Not only will you meet neighbors, but some of your shoppers may tell you about an item they have to sell that might be just what you have been wanting to buy. Now you have a chance to get it at a bargain price.

Your In-House Advertising

First of all, do all your advertising at least five days before your sale. Be sure to ask for permission to post signs at certain locations. Usually ten dollars to the superintendent will produce considerable cooperation for what you plan to do. If you live in a substantial middle-class apartment house, be sure you double the lubricant fee.

Get permission to post signs at the mail boxes. Elevators are usually out of bounds for announcements, but certainly inquire about the possibility. If you cannot use the elevators to promote your sale, try to get permission to have signs placed on a wall near the elevators in the lobby.

With an adequate amount of green cheer, you might get the approval of your doorman to place a box filled with your flyers at the table near the entrance. Staple a small sign on the box stating: For Your Information.

Leave a sign and a box of flyers in the laundry room. If you have a spirited commitment to reach everyone in your apartment complex, slip a copy of the flyer under every door. For five dollars you can get a dependable youngster who will do the job. If you're worried about having your notices dumped, distribute them yourself. If a door opens, introduce yourself. It's really fun.

Inviting the Public

You might decide at the outset that your potential customer yield from your apartment house might not be enough to sell out all the merchandise you have. You would then have to open up your sale to the public, but on a controlled basis.

The following is a list of locations in your community where your posters and flyers will do the most good:

1. Your church or temple bulletin board
2. The community board of your supermarket
3. Your beauty shop
4. The neighborhood nursery
5. A nearby restaurant where you regularly dine and have befriended the owner
6. The community bulletin board at your local library

Think of other merchants you know who might cooperate in allowing you to put a sign in their window, on the inside counter, or on a wall of their stores. Don't assume you will be refused. Pleasant surprises come by making efforts and inquiries and from refusing to accept defeat.

Crowd Control

Now more than ever you need the benevolence of your door-man and superintendent. Inform them when the sale will be held—let's say a Saturday from 10:00 A.M. to 4:00 P.M. Pay the pipers to keep everything agreeable and harmonious.

Have two friends or aides at the door throughout to monitor the traffic flow. They should have numbered cards to give to shoppers who must wait their turn to get into the lobby and up the elevator. Depending on the size of your apartment, allow only six to ten people in at a time. In this way you can answer queries fully and take the time to describe the furniture and other merchandise for sale.

Have at least two people assisting you and serving as general security. Lock rooms that have nothing for sale in them. If the doors to these rooms have no locks, use masking tape to close them. Do the same to your kitchen cabinets. People will look into everything, so shut off out-of-bounds areas.

Advertising Your Sale

If you are not partial to crowds, the stress of bargaining, and the general press of people meandering through your apartment, you can advertise to sell your unwanted merchandise. This is a calmer, more civilized undertaking.

Place a classified ad specifically listing what you have to sell. For smaller items specify a category—household tools, kitchen utensils, china, and bathroom accessories. Just list your telephone number.

When you are called, describe your wares more fully and listen carefully to get a reading of the caller. Certainly, with some conversation, you will be able to conclude if you have a genuinely interested consumer, a curiosity seeker, or simply a no-good. If you find a person is really interested and would like to see what you are selling, then you make an appointment to have that individual come to your apartment.

The advertising can keep you at home at some inconvenient times to meet with buyers, but it does eliminate that consumer crush that is characteristic of one or two day sales. It's what suits you best that matters.

THE BLOCK SALE

Block sales, where several families on a single street decide to sell their clutter at the same time, can be orchestrated into outdoor festivals. Food vendors can be invited to be present, the street can be decorated colorfully, and music can be piped outside for the pleasure of the customers. Block sales usually are held in neighborhoods that have one- and two-family homes.

Merchandise is displayed on tables outside the house. Even large pieces should be brought outdoors and placed on the sidewalk. If tables are scarce, spread your wares out on a blanket and let the street become your sale emporium.

Done in tandem with your neighbors, no one will object to the display of "junk." For those who participate, it will be a profitable day. For those who decide against participating in this joint project, it still can be a fun event. But there are important guidelines to follow in order to maintain harmony in the neighborhood.

To organize a block sale, you will have to initiate the project by inviting all the neighbors on the block to a meeting to discuss it. Do not pass anyone by, even if you are certain that a family would not join in your block sale. Avoid troublesome opposition by inviting everyone to participate. People who do not want to participate actively in the sale might like to contribute pieces to be sold.

Decide on sale dates at least four weeks ahead. In this way everyone will have ample time to find items to sell, and the group will have time to prepare signs and place an ad in the local paper.

Now the chief coordinator of this operation, along with another member of the group, must go to the police department to get a permit to display merchandise on the street. You might also request permission to close the street to traffic during the sale.

At a block sale, each family becomes an individual merchant with their own tables and displays. Use your kitchen, dining room, and bridge tables to display merchandise. If some people need additional tables, they can be rented inexpensively from caterers.

Advertise your sale as a Block Sale Festival. All families should decorate their homes with colorful pennants. This attracts the attention of passing pedestrians and motorists unaware of your block sale. Put speakers outside and fill the street with background music. Invite street vendors who sell hot dogs, ice cream, and even more sophisticated food (shish kebob wagons are found all over midtown Manhattan) to your sale. Most will come as they already have their vendors' permits and are looking for high traffic locations. If you do arrange for food to be sold at your block sale, include this information on your signs and in your advertisement: Enjoy Delicious Snacks.

Remember to post your homemade flyers at every appropriate place to attract more shoppers. With careful planning and advertising, your block sale will be fun and profitable.

DISPLAYING MERCHANDISE

When food is served that is appealing to the eye, it becomes more pleasurable to the palate. The same is true of your merchandise. Good looking displays attract shoppers and loosen pocketbooks.

Jill Goldstone of the Garage Sale Store said, "Every piece I sell has its own place on the shelf, giving it a sense of importance whether it is tagged for 25¢ or $25." You might not have the room to give every item such display space, but never crowd merchandise together. You must establish a sense of orderliness and product visibility that will catch the shopper's eye. This, as you can understand, invites inspection that can become consideration and then develop into a sale.

Badly stacked merchandise is a consumer turn-off. Your precious, potential purchasers who have stopped at your sale will breeze by and then out. This is especially true of the substantial number of impulse buyers not looking for anything special, just for something of interest.

Remember, if your merchandise looks like it has just escaped the garbage, that is what you will get for your wares.

DISPLAY TIPS

1. Use every available table in your house for your sale, including picnic and card tables. For extra display space, you can remove the door in the basement and set it up to accommodate items.

2. Cover all tables with a colorful cloth: bedsheets, tablecloths, even plastic ones, that have seen their best days. Enhance your merchandise.

3. Clean china and glassware. A soiled lawnmower has some bargain appeal, but dirty dishes just create sales resistance.

4. Jewelry, coin collections, and other small valuables that can be pocketed by people with nimble fingers should be in some glass or lucite container. Show these to shoppers upon request.

5. Precious Hummel figures, Dresden figurines, and other valuables of this type should be placed at the back of the tables. Customers can reach over to handle them and you can maintain the necessary vigilance.

6. Display such items as doillies, lace, shawls, and quilts by hanging or tacking them on a wall of your house. These items will also bring higher prices if they are cleaned.

7. Display tools, machinery, and garden equipment in the garage. Male shoppers will go directly to this area in search of what they need. While there are many men who come to browse, most usually know exactly what they want.

8. Display clothes on a rented pipe rack. Your best bet for a rental is from a catering hall. Clothes racks are available particularly during the warm weather months when overcoats are idling away in closets until winter.

9. Improvise a line to hold clothes by suspending a tight rope between two convenient places. Even better, use a long dog chain instead and hang garments in the loops. This prevents

garments from slipping down into an unsightly mass in the middle, a problem that can occur with rope.

10. Arrange to have a full-length mirror secured to a wall, away from the traffic flow, where consumers can try on clothes and see themselves. Would you buy a jacket, coat, or sweater without trying it on and looking into a mirror to see if you approve of your prospective purchase? Of course not!

11. It is always more effective selling to show furniture in the setting of your home, but it is more advisable to keep strangers out of your house. Too many security precautions would be needed. Display your big pieces outside in an open area just away from your tables. Since these are your higher priced items, a place away from the crowd allows people to inspect each piece leisurely.

12. Use boxes to display records, books, baby clothes, bric-a-brac, and broken products of any kind that can be bought for parts. Stack books with the titles showing and allow enough room in the boxes of records for people to flip through your offerings.

CUSTOMER COAXING

You're exposed to customer coaxing every day of your life. You see it to annoyance on television when your senses are jarred by those mindless commercials. You find it in newspapers and magazines. It's simply professional persuasion.

How can you use it at your sale? With the kind of subtle wisdom that delivers more sales and commands higher prices. Every shopper, the marketing experts determined long ago, likes to have purchasing reassurance. You see and hear it all of the time. This cleaner is now "new and improved." The competitor then claims its product now "fights dirt 25 percent better." The unanswered question is, "twenty-five percent better than what?"

You can use product-hype to move your merchandise at your sale. Along with your price tag, use a little salesmanship. Place a sign on your lawnmower that says, "Easy to Operate" or "Starts Fast" or "Excellent Cutting." Pick the one you prefer; do not over do it. On the vacuum cleaner, put a sign that reads, "Powerful Cleaner," and on the couch, "Solid Frame." If you are selling a garment with a designer name, make it known. Attach a tag that says, "Designer Label." A good standard is, "Hardly Used." The big ticket items are worth this extra effort.

DISPLAY PRICES

For items that have a hard surface, simply mark the price on a self-adhering label and put it in a conspicuous place. The first thing shoppers look for after instant interest in an item is the price. While labels look neater, masking tape is a good substitute.

Pieces like furniture, lawnmowers, and chain saws are best displayed with a hang tag showing the price. Use a hang tag for suits, dresses, coats, and all sizeable garments. For small soft goods from clothes to linens, staple labels to each piece.

CUSTOMER CONVENIENCE

Provide all the things you get in a store when you make a purchase for your customers.

Paper bags—People, even at garage sales, like their purchases bagged

Boxes—for shoppers who buy a substantial number of items

String and cord—for tying packages

Tape measure—for people who want to note the size of couch, coffee table, and any other large item

Extension cord—attached to an electrical outlet in the house to be used by people who want to test appliances. (All of your electrical products must be in good working order; otherwise they should be sold for parts.)

Dolly—a welcome aid to shoppers who have to cart away refrigerators, washers, dryers, and other products of this type

Heavy rope—to secure large pieces to cars

SECURITY

You need security—today more than ever. While there has always been an expected number of light-fingered shoppers, theft is rampant nationwide and occurs at every sale.

Having relatives or friends assigned to directing the traffic flow and discreetly watching shoppers as they remove items to inspect them is essential. Most often, small pieces displayed at the front of your table vanish suddenly.

To minimize incidents of theft, place self-adhering stickers on all of your sales assistants identifying each of them as a sale attendant. When people know they are being monitored, they curb their impulse to take freebees. If your security force really appears to be directing people to merchandise they want to see—like floorwalkers—you can avoid giving your legitimate shoppers the uncomfortable sensation that they are being watched.

Carol Kiley, who winces at the inevitability of losing merchandise to larcenous browsers, recommends an effective way of avoiding an unpleasant confrontation when you see a person taking something. Carol goes to the shopper and says, "Excuse me, but I need to check the price of that piece you plan to buy."

Because the shopper is utterly startled by this swift approach of an official of the sale, the item taken is usually produced immediately. After Carol proceeds with her mock check-out, and returns the item to the person, it is put back on the table.

What happens if the customer claims nothing was taken? "If the item is small and not too expensive," Carol advises, "let this shopper have it, and then tell the person to leave immediately. The thief will depart quickly."

What if an expensive piece is taken? Obviously, this cannot be overlooked with benevolent indulgence. Carol's action remedy is a polite but heated warning, "Either you return what you took or I'll call the police." Does it work? It never fails. Most of these people are as concerned about being involved in an unpleasant scene as you are about making one.

However, as efficient as your security might be, expect several pieces to be missing when the sale is over. For many people, thievery is not only a practice, but an art form.

FIGURE 8. For items that have a hard surface, mark the price on a self-sticking label and put it in a conspicuous place.

FIGURE 9. Best way to price such ornate items would be to attach a hang tag to the handles.

FIGURE 10. Quick conversion. Books instead of tools were stacked on these shelves during this garage sale. Neatly lettered sign clearly provides customers with price information.

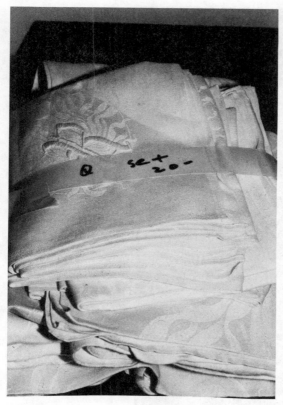

FIGURE 11. Linens should be assorted into sets when displayed for sale. The number of pieces is noted on the masking tape band.

FIGURE 12. Self-adhering label is used to price chair.

FIGURE 13. Assorted bric-a-brac can be offered for sale from open cartons.

PRICING

The standard rule at any kind of sale of used merchandise is to set an asking price that you will put on your labels and tags and have a lower selling price firmly fixed in your mind. If you are a person with compulsive integrity and frown on this programmed overpricing, set your conscience at ease.

Patrons of homestyle sales are practiced bargainers. Even more important, they *expect* to pay less than the asking price. Of course, you should not mark up any item outrageously. This is an instant turn-off for shoppers as they will be discouraged from entering into hopeful negotiation to have the price reduced, making the piece an attractive buy.

Set guidelines for yourself to make it easy for you to remember what your selling price is. Take $10 off merchandise tagged from $40–$50; from $60–$100, allow for a discount of up to $15; above $100, prepare to drop the price down reluctantly during the inevitable bargaining sessions about $25. You might not have to reduce it that much. A rare impulse buyer will pay the tag price; others will settle somewhere in between what you have asked and what you will take.

FREQUENTLY ASKED QUESTIONS

Here are questions asked most often by people planning their first garage sale:

How Do I Know What to Charge for My Merchandise?

You have to find the going market price for your item at the time you hold your sale. The best bet is to do some comparison shopping. Make a list of the products you will be selling and price them at about a half dozen garage sales in your area. Do not limit your price exploration to the yard sales only. Stop in at estate and home contents sales being conducted by professionals. After you have noted the prices asked, you will come up with a good average for all of your items. "What a piece is really worth is what you get for it in the marketplace," said Jill Goldstone. Carol Kiley added, "Condition matters very much."

What About Brand New, Unused Merchandise I Will Be Selling?

Check the prices at department stores and other shops to see what the same products cost now. This will not be nearly what you will get selling your suitcase or lamp in the driveway of your house. Tag your pieces at one-third the cost of new merchandise. Be prepared to have the price pierced by patrons. As you know, nothing sells for the asking price. One lady offered to pay $12 for a $40 Samsonite suitcase actually taken right out of the box. Declining the bid, the owner sold it the second day of the weekend sale for eight dollars.

How Do I Price My Antiques?

Take your treasures to antique dealers. If they are large pieces, such as furniture, dealers will come to your house or apartment.

As Jill Goldstone points out, "Dealers will offer you about one-third the value of your antiques. Your sixteenth century vase might be worth $1,200, but you will be offered about $450 for it. Ultimately, the dealer will sell the vase for its full market value. However, he might have to hold it for several months to make the sale."

You have almost nothing to lose by placing the piece for sale at your sell-a-thon at $700. Some amateur antique hunter, aware of its dealer value, might buy it for $650 or $600. Whatever you make above the $450 dealer price is your bonus. If the piece does not sell, then the dealer will happily take it off your hands for $450.

Should I Take Bids
for Important Pieces?

Having established your bottom price for a living room set in fine condition, do not surrender your bargaining position too quickly. If a customer is willing to pay less than your firm bottom price, have that person fill out a bid card. The information to be filled in is address, telephone number, and how much that person is willing to pay for the set. (See the sample bid card at the end of this chapter.) Before the sale ends, tell the people who made the highest bid that they can have the merchandise. Frequently, people will have changed their minds. Then keep going down the list, phoning others who offered the next highest price, until you get a customer who is ready to take your living room set away. You will have to call hardly more than a few interested buyers.

Should I Take a Deposit
on a High-Priced Item?

Yes, but keep taking the names and addresses of interested buyers whom you can call if the sale is not completed. The deposit will insure a phone call from you, informing the prospective buyer that the item will be sold to someone else unless he or she comes back to pay in full.

How Long Should I Keep My Bottom Price Firm?

Until the afternoon of the last day of the sale; then slash the prices of everything 50 percent. There are shoppers who come to sales at this time knowing that the half price reduction will take place automatically. Of course, these people know that the best merchandise has already been sold. They look for super bargains among the remainders.

What Do I Do If a Person Switches a Price Tag?

Price switching is a practice of some garage sale shoppers. It is the bargain mentality con. Take the time to make a master list of all the merchandise for sale. Exclude anything costing a dollar or less.

When a $50 crystal bowl is suddenly being checked out with a $20 price tag, just look at your master list for verification and then tell the customer, "Sorry, but according to my price list that piece should be $50. It was tagged incorrectly." If the shopper protests, the Tag-Along-Girls take the piece and declare, "Sorry, it's not for sale."

Sonny Kiley uses a special shock treatment technique. Looking at the obviously switched $20 tag and then checking his master list, Sonny will exclaim, "That's all wrong. That piece should be marked $85." Confused by the disclosure that the item costs $35 more than the price on the original tag, the patron leaves the piece and quickly vanishes.

One recommended solution, which takes more time than most weekend merchants care to devote to the tedious task, is to simply note what each item is: China Bowl, $15; Pressure Cooker, $20; Glass Tray, $22.50.

Can I Offer Any Incentives
to Shoppers?

Yes, you can sell merchandise in "packages" to heighten sales appeal. The person bargaining hard for the television set but refusing to meet your bottom price might accept an attractive combination offer of the TV set and a table available to accommodate it.

When you suggest the purchase of two related items, think of getting what you had expected for both. Books, records, and toys boxed for display can be offered at combination rates: 25¢ each or three for 55¢. Package sales move merchandise.

Here are some additional pricing tips:

Mark the prices in bold, large letters as an aid to senior citizens and other people who do not see well.

Place price tags where they will be found easily. If you do not have a staple gun, use a safety pin to attach tags to clothes or linens.

If you are eager to make a sale and the offering price is not too far below your bottom line, take it.

Remain firm with fine merchandise until the last day of your sale. Good stuff will sell. To get rid of leftovers, contact local second-hand stores. While the buy-out price for everything might seem low to you, it will be worth it to get your castoffs carted away.

If you plan another sale in the future, keep your remaining merchandise.

Basic Price Guide

Baby carriage	Strollers, $20; Full-size, $30
Baskets	$1–$5
Bicycles	$25; 10 speed, $80
Boxspring and mattress	$30
Chairs	$50–$90

China	$1–$100, depending on condition, maker, and how much of a set remains
Clocks	$5
Clothing	Dress, $2; Men's suit, $15; Coats, $15
Couch	$40
Crib	$45
Desk	$20
Dishwasher	$50
Electric drill	$5
Freezer, upright	$115
Glassware	Ordinary, 50¢
High chair	$20
Hand mower	$5
Lawnmower, power	$40
Linens	Sheets, $1; Pillow cases, 50¢; Bath towels, large $1; Blankets, wool, $13
Playpen	$15
Pots and pans	$1
Pressure cooker	$8
Radio	$5-$10
Refrigerator-freezer	$125
Rugs	$10 and up
Sewing machine	$50
Silverware	Pieces, 10–15¢; Silverplate set, $10
Tables	$25; Oak, $50
Tennis racket	Metal, $20; Wood, $5
Toys and games	$1 each
TV	Five years old or less, black and white, $35; Color table, $100; Console, $130
Washing machine	$90 for one less than five years old and in good condition

```
┌─────────────────────────────────────────────────────┐
│                                                     │
│                    TAG ALONG                        │
│                   INDIAN TRAIL                      │
│              HARRISON, NEW YORK 10528               │
│                                                     │
│                  MERCHANDISE BID                    │
│     Dear Customer,                                  │
│       We will be glad to accept your bid, but please remember │
│     that we take you seriously and expect you to honor your │
│     bid.                                            │
│                                                     │
│     ITEM:                                           │
│                                                     │
│     PRICE MARKED:                                   │
│                                                     │
│     BID:                                            │
│                                                     │
│     NAME:                                           │
│                                                     │
│     PHONE:                                          │
│                                                     │
└─────────────────────────────────────────────────────┘
```

FIGURE 14. Here is a sample bid card used by the Tag-Along Girls.

MONEY
MANAGEMENT

The success or failure of a movie is measured by the results at the box office. A triumph for your private enterprise is determined by the size of your profits when the sale is over. So remember, your money container will be exposed to a steady stream of shoppers. Blended into the congestion that will swell and then thin out during your mercantile event will be larcenous lookers who see the cash box as the prize catch at the sale. Carelessly guarded, your profits can vanish as quickly as a speck of dust blown into the winds.

THE CHECKOUT

Set up a checkout table about 15 feet away from the main display area, in a place where people will pass it on their way out. This provides additional security and is a convenience for patrons who want to pay for their purchases as they leave. It should be identified with a sizeable sign saying: Pay Here. Don't forget that you will need to make change for early customers. Start with about 15 singles, 6 fives, 2 tens, and an ample supply of nickels, dimes, and quarters.

Use a metal box to hold your change and the cash received for purchased items. Always keep the money in the box with the lid down. Do not use any kind of container that puts your escalating wealth in sight of the public. This only invites its premature departure, not only by a nimble adult whose pockets are already filled with some of your smaller items, but also by a seemingly playful child who thinks your transparent container is an attractive toy. In fact, the youngster might be responding to parental instruction about how they would appreciate having your treasure trough at home. Somewhat Dickensian, but it is being done.

Never in your lovely community, you think? It happens everywhere and not just to local merchants, department stores, and supermarkets. "Theft," cautions the Kileys, who have seen some inventive thievery during their 20 years of conducting garage sales professionally, "is inevitable. You must expect to find that many things will be taken."

However, with care, it should never be your cash box.

USE TWO PEOPLE

One person can handle the cash box most of the time, but having two people at the checkout table is a wise investment in person-power. Two people can keep a checkout line from becoming discouragingly long. Many impatient shoppers, planning to drop in on a few sales in one day, will be tempted to leave an impulse purchase rather than face any kind of long wait to pay. Double-teaming will keep the checkout functioning without interruption should one person have to leave for any reason.

Two people monitoring the cash flow prevents the proceeds from suddenly disappearing when one person is busy making change, when the box is obscured by merchandise placed on the table, or when one person is distracted answering a patron's question.

REDUCE YOUR HOLDINGS

As the box fills with cash, keep reducing the amount kept in the metal container. In fact, never allow it to become full. Keep what you need to make change. Have a member of the two-person team bring the cash into the house, where it will be hidden safely.

When you are paid with any bill from five dollars and up, adopt the technique professional cashiers use. Place the bill down on the side of the box where both you and the customer can see it. If the purchase is for $3.50, then lift the lid of the box, remove $1.50. Then pick up the five dollar bill and put it into the cash box.

This is a standard technique used to reassure customers who forget what size bill they gave to you. Often they will think it was higher than the one they used to make the payment. This is usually an honest shopper gaff. By keeping the bill visible until the transaction is concluded, there is no reason to challenge the change. Note how professionals never put a large bill away until the change is made. Somehow the visible payment technique is more reassuring to shoppers. If the large bill never leaves their sight, it is a "customer comfort."

If you prefer not to risk putting the bill down on the table, especially when the checkout is extremely busy, then a man can stick the bill into his shirt pocket, where half of it can be seen at all times; a woman can do the same by wearing a blouse that has a pocket.

Another option commonly used by the change makers is

to announce the size of the bill when it is given. Simply say aloud, "Three-fifty out of five," or "Seven dollars out of ten."

TAKING CHECKS

Professionals interviewed overwhelmingly said, "Yes, take a check." "Cash only" sales immediately reduce attendance by suggesting an untrusting attitude to the public. While shoplifting is an acknowledged fact, so is the reality that nearly all shoppers are honorable people.

But there are still some safety guidelines to follow. Set a minimum amount for a check, as stores do for credit card purchases. Make it for at least $20, as it is reasonable for you to expect to be paid in cash for purchases costing less.

However, do not be rigid. If by late afternoon a shopper offers to pay by check for a purchase amounting to $15, explaining that all his or her cash was used at other tag sales, you can be flexible.

YOUR SAFETY GUIDE

Don't drop your minimum below ten dollars.

Ask for a driver's license for identification.

If a customer says he or she doesn't drive, ask for credit cards. Note the number. Always be sure to get something that gives you the person's home address and that the identification cards offered have not expired.

If the sum is considerable, take down the license plate number of the buyer's car.

Never take checks above the amount of the purchase.

Do not be casual. Look carefully at signatures. If not satisfied, ask for additional identification.

Record the following information: name and address, telephone number, credit card numbers, and possibly a license plate number.

FIGURE 15. Judy Sclier of the Tag-Along Girls demonstrates why a casually managed cash box brimming with bills is such a prize catch for larcenous shoppers.

HANDLING CUSTOMERS AND TRAFFIC

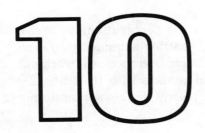

Ambiance is not just an atmospheric character evaluation of restaurants. Nearly everything projects some kind of chill or charm. Corporations spend millions of dollars having their advertising agencies create "product personality."

The instant people step into your yard or your driveway, they are met with an aura that establishes the thrust of your sale: friendly, casual, indifferent, or cold. Salespeople controlling the impulse to discuss merchandise can appear grim, creating a frosty atmosphere. On the other hand, the barker-like product hustler reassuring you that there are great buys to be found is equally objectionable.

Indifference is generated by the people running the sale when they sit around in clusters, chatting animatedly to each other and ignoring customers. Tentative beginners will work out their nervousness in conversational confabs with their working colleagues when they should be ready to answer customer queries.

SOME BEHAVIOR GUIDELINES

1. Use a sign that immediately projects a warm welcome: Thank You for Coming.

2. Be attentive. When a customer is examining a product, volunteer additional information. "That was made in 1910; if you look underneath, you'll see it's from Tiffany."

3. Suggest a product use that is not always obvious. "This vase would make a lovely lamp," "That container would make an attractive flower box," or "That beautiful bedspread could also be made into drapes."

4. If you see a person interested in an item but hesitant to examine it, gently inquire, "Would you like to look at this jewelry box?" Then pick it up to hand it to the customer and add a historical footnote. "I bought this when we vacationed in Mexico six years ago."

TRAFFIC CONTROL

Traffic congestion can be a problem. Clogged rural roads reduced to just one passable lane can be dangerous. Blocked driveways along with double parked cars on suburban streets can bring angry protests from neighbors and rupture the friendly relationships. Here are some tips for traffic control:

1. Arrange to have someone at the sale assigned to monitoring motorists during the most hectic periods, as determined shoppers will snare *any* parking space to get close to your house.

2. Place signs at the curb near each of your next door neighbors' driveways that say, "Do not block driveway." This will create lasting goodwill between you and the people in your neighborhood.

3. When an uncaring customer puts his car in the driveway anyway, have your traffic controller get the license plate number and announce at the sale that this car must be moved.

4. Keep enough space cleared around your house for shoppers who must cart away large pieces. They will, of course, need to drive as close to the sale area as possible.

5. When the traffic gets extremely heavy, have your motorist monitor guide cars in, out, and away from your sale site.

6. Tight rural roads become extremely hazardous when lines of cars reduce the traveling space to one lane. Use two traffic controllers to create a safe vehicle flow under these circumstances. To accommodate cars driving to the sale, station one person at the entrance to the sale to signal when cars can exit and another down the road to stop incoming autos until the roadway is cleared.

7. Use red flags at both control points to effectively halt traffic when necessary.

To keep traffic from developing into a car crunch, you must be prepared to control it.

MULTI-FAMILY SALE

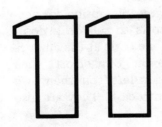

With the growing popularity of the home merchandise mart in suburbia, the lone, yard sale entrepreneur faces considerable competition nearly everywhere. To offset the glut of weekend sales bidding for customers, the trend is to merge merchandise and people-power to create a giant sell-a-thon that will truly attract shoppers. It is the multifamily sale, where the quantity of trash-treasures is a big consumer lure. The unity of three families means a triple bounty at a single stop. This type of sales togetherness in the city is called a "block sale."

Joining a multifamily sale is an agreeable option for people who just do not have enough castoffs to sell on a do-it-yourself basis. Yet, ample stuff to stack one table at the alliance of homeowners is all that is needed for the joint effort. Then there are people who have some remainders left from their own sales that they would like to convert into cash. They are also good candidates for the togetherness sale.

POTENTIAL PROBLEMS

Susan Posmentier of Croton-on-Hudson, New York, has organized multifamily sales for several years. She observes that, "We not only get much more merchandise, but we can display it better by holding the sale at the home of the family with the biggest yard or the longest driveway. And, if you get cooperative neighbors to join in, it can be fun. In fact, I have always found it a profitable social occasion."

But it also can be a disruptive experience for once friendly neighbors, according to Carol Kiley. "The families who join in can become very envious of each other," she pointed out. "When one family sells more than the next one, you can hear some people grumbling about how they would have sold everything if they held their own sale."

Hard feelings and resentment can easily surface at a multifamily sale, agrees Susan. "A big source of irritation," she emphasized, "is when people drift away from their own tables to have chit-chats with the neighbors, instead of watching the traffic and helping to sell."

Resentment develops frequently at the close of the weekend merchandise marathon when it is time to clean up and move out. Some people will take their wares and leave without making any effort to tidy up the grounds. Others forget to fold up the tables loaned to them by the host family or fail to remove those they own. One lady, a veteran of many multifamily sales, said she would have to call her neighbors repeatedly afterward before the abandoned tables were moved out of her yard.

HOW TO AVOID CONFLICT

1. Screen your neighbors with great care.
2. Establish working guidelines for pricing. Inflated

89

price tags will turn off customers. Realistic pricing is essential to the success of your sale for bargain hunters.

3. Decide whether you will have individual tables with each family selling their own merchandise or put everything together.

4. If you opt for the togetherness approach, display merchandise in related groups: tools, clothes, appliances. Have one checkout table, and then determine how the cash flow is to be monitored. Use different colored tags to represent each family or ones with the family initials on them. Either technique will make it fairly easy to tabulate each participant's earnings at the end of the sale.

5. Since the tag shows the asking price, mark the actual amount received for the item on each tag when a sale is made.

6. Insist that all families have everything ready for display the night before the sale. Keep merchandise locked up indoors, but be ready to get everything out in time for your 9:00 A.M. opening. Figure two hours for the outside work.

7. Do not leave merchandise outside unattended overnight. If you do, expect much to be gone by morning.

8. Anticipate every conceivable contingency, such as duplicate items being sold. Obviously, the less expensive ones will sell first. To avoid friction, you can agree to display them one at a time. Make every decision possible in advance to minimize the stress that can develop during a collective effort.

9. Short memories fire quick tempers. Take the time to write out the ground rules and distribute a copy to everyone. Should any quarrel arise, check the written word for guidance. This eliminates the problem of anybody saying, "I don't remember agreeing to that."

10. If any prospective participant appears to be agreeing reluctantly to the guidelines being formulated, politely ask that person to drop out. Explain that maintaining a friendship is understandably more important than arranging a sale.

11. Decide on your security force. Some muscular husbands clearly tagged "Garage Sale Information" will dramatically reduce your losses by theft.

12. No matter how eager everyone is to get the sale underway, do not admit early birds. Keep to the advertised opening time. Your reputation for dependability will prompt your customers to come back to your next multifamily sale.

People who plan their joint-family sales with the thoroughness required to maintain harmony among the happy hucksters find this type of selling a fun experience.

HOME
CONTENTS
SALE

Selling the contents of a home is a massive project that would be an extremely ambitious undertaking for the amateur. This is the time to call in a professional. When the cash is finally counted, you will have made more leaving it to the pro than doing it yourself.

Judy Sclier, the spokesperson for Tag-Along Girls, four experts who can sell almost everything in a house within three days, explains just one way a pro can increase your profit margin. "During the many years we have coordinated sales, we have never failed to find something a couple or individual thought was worthless but we knew immediately could be sold for as much as $1,500."

Spotting these profitable pieces with a trained eye is one thing; the other is finding them beneath the piles of castoffs stuck away in the most foul recesses of damp basements and musty attics. There is a chorus of screams when the mice come scurrying out of their cozy corners and holes. Once the Tag-Along Girls had to dislodge some snakes that were nesting in a rarely used summer home.

"When we got this house," Judy remembers, "we were so unimpressed with it that we were sorry we took the job. But, you know, it is always possible to find treasure in trash, and that's what makes this business so exciting. We retrieved an old lamp that was put on the garbage pile for pick-up and there was our treasure. It was a valuable, genuine antique."

DIGGING FOR TREASURE

The Tag-Along Girls are like archeological explorers who dig for precious finds in their own special terrain: attics, closets, crawlspaces, garages, and basements. This is a tiresome effort that few people would have the patience to do as thoroughly in their own homes. It is an unappetizing undertaking, inspecting assorted discards that have become moldy mounds of junk.

"I think that's why many people call us in," smiled Judy. "They have the attitude of 'let the girls clean up that garbage.' It's really a filthy job—looking at every single piece of merchandise—some of it untouched for years."

Yet, Judy points out, this is a kind of modern day gold mining expedition. "As pros, we are not impatient," she continued. "We know that those dusty tables, chairs, old china, and other things can be sold."

The quartet is highly committed to these search-and-discover missions, which are the first stages of preparing for a home contents sale. If they have the slightest suspicion that any find might have special value, it is reviewed at least three times by the entire group before it is tagged with a price.

When they found a pair of dentures, they first chuckled and then cheered. They all saw the gold in the abandoned bridgework. At that time the precious metal was selling for over $700 an ounce. They sold the dentures.

EXPERTISE MATTERS

How do they make these product evaluations? Seasoning and experience help, but the four women started by learning their profession and then sharpened their skills by practicing it. All of the partners have taken such courses as American and European Furniture, American-Continental Antiques, Art Valuables from 1690–1830, and courses dealing with valuables of later periods.

Added to this formidable background, the ladies, all under 40 years of age, studied precious metals and then learned all about collectibles. "In this way," said Judy, "you don't guess but *know* the value beneath the dust."

MAILING LIST

If you are still debating whether to do-it-yourself or turn your home sale over to the pros, here is another factor to consider. After conducting sales every weekend from early spring to late fall, and then proceeding to do the same for apartments during the winter, the group has developed a large following of patrons. These customers are sophisticated buyers, many looking for special pieces of furniture, china, or collectibles.

The Tag-Along-Girls have noted their clients' preferences on file cards. When they undertake a sale and have completed assorting and cleaning the items to be sold, they check their customer mailing lists for the best buyers to invite. Then a flyer about the sale is mailed to these home contents shoppers. "Our following is so faithful," according to Judy, "that the mailing alone brings out a sizeable number of people."

Of course, they also use all the other promotional techniques, from putting up signs to advertising locally to pull customer traffic from the community. With this kind of professional clout and the ability to discover those costly castoffs that many people might be too embarrassed to put up for sale, the professionals appear to be worth their 10 to 20 percent commission. The commission depends on the amount of merchandise to be sold.

Actually, the professionals offer a no-risk service to the seller. The home contents sales pros do all of the work: cleaning, display, advertising, crowd control, and supplying the aids needed to help sell and provide the necessary security. They pay for all the promotions and advertising and are responsible for bad checks. They make up the loss.

TIPS FOR DO-IT-YOURSELFERS

If you are still committed to doing it yourself, here are some tips from the Tag-Along Girls:

1. Check everything—including the pockets of your clothes.
2. Consider the condition of an item when setting the price.
3. Capitalize on the big demand for furniture.
4. Never paint furniture. The worn oak pieces will sell better as they are.
5. Look for names on old pieces: Tiffany, Lalique, Hummel, and well-known artists.
6. Be aware that the most saleable items are the practical and usable ones: glass, silverware, rugs, chairs, tools, pots, and pans.
7. Polish Sterling silver until it sparkles. There should be no black on any of it. Polish copper. Bronze needs less attention.
8. Do not restore damaged pieces as it then becomes difficult to mark up price enough to make a profit.
9. Display such "in-demand" merchandise as handmade items, fine linens and tableclothes, and all kinds of dolls.

10. Tape all your closet doors shut, as people will look into everything.

11. Close off rooms that are not being used for the sale. Still, don't be surprised to find some tired senior citizen dozing in your bedroom. Some people will push taped but unlocked doors open.

12. Have a security salesperson in every room.

13. Take bids for high-priced merchandise if no one has offered you your selling price.

14. Tag items with your asking price, which is expected to be reduced.

15. Give shoppers one sales slip. Each time they buy something, note the purchase on the slip. The total amount due will be tabulated at the checkout.

16. Locate your cash box at the door to catch the traffic

FIGURE 16. Preparing to conduct a home contents sale, the Tag-Along Girls bring their own checkout table, order pads, bid cards, self-sticking labels used to make price changes, paper bags, masking tape, a thermos full of coffee, and a carton full of sandwiches.

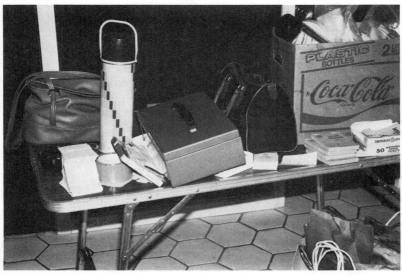

coming out. This is where shoppers will pay for purchases marked on the sales slip.

17. House contents sales draw tremendous traffic. If necessary, have a uniformed guard to control the flow of cars.

18. Keep your master list of merchandise handy at the checkout as you must always watch out for tag switchers.

19. Do not put your phone number in your ad, as you will be pestered by callers who want to come early to see what you are selling.

20. Insist that people who buy big items, such as furniture, pay in advance and make arrangements for pick-up.

21. Yes, take checks.

Now, you can decide whether you can expect to make more money by doing it yourself or by using the professionals.

FIGURE 17. Holding her order pad, cheerful Hesta Fortgang, greets customers and answers their queries. She also serves as the security monitor for the room.

FIGURE 18. Annemarie Gordon writing up a purchase. Small items are displayed in a case where they can be watched more easily.

FIGURE 19. At this home contents sale for a man who owned a men's wear shop, new shirts from the store were placed on sale.

FIGURE 20. Tape all doors shut to keep traffic out of rooms not being used for the sale.

FUND RAISING SALE

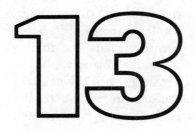

The coffers of charities and churches need to be replenished continually. When the national economy dips and increasing numbers of people throughout the country are straining to pay their bills, contributions to good causes become sparse. Faced with the obvious fact that even noble deeds cannot continue without money, benevolent organizations must turn to fund raising.

Now these worthy institutions competing to coax cash from struggling and often strapped supporters must contend with a relatively new entrant into the ranks of the penniless petitioners. Cities in crisis verging on the precipice of bankruptcy have been cheered by the earnings made by holding mammoth garage sales. Today, it is a necessity of survival.

While most municipalities can manage until the next tax payments come in, goodwill organizations are not so readily indulged by creditors. The urgent need for money must be met.

HOLD A SALE

Since people prefer to shop at a sale that has a massive amount of merchandise than hop-scotch from house to house during a weekend, organizational fund-raising events attract heavy traffic. The church yard, the nursery playground, or a section of a large hospital parking lot make excellent areas to accommodate giant garage sales.

Organizations can easily rally an ample supply of workers, from muscle to management, who can be organized to orchestrate a profitable sale.

GETTING MERCHANDISE

Saleable junk is waiting to be plucked from the basements, attics, and garages of people who want nothing better than to have it picked up and taken away. Some towns provide a special carting service several times a year expressly for large pieces: chairs, tables, sofas, television sets, and anything else too big to be put into a garbage can.

Pure junk, you think? Hardly. Mitch Goldstone, who moonlights at his wife's Garage Sale Store, carefully reviews these roadside throw-aways before the town truck carts them away.

"What treasures we find!" enthused Mitch. "People don't know what they're tossing out."

These people really don't care. They don't have the temperament or interest to hold a tag sale. They just want to get rid of their discards. At one time many people called the Salvation Army first. But this honorable organization, traditionally ready to pick up almost anything, is now more selective in what it takes.

While cast offs that can be converted into needed cash

are literally waiting to be taken, few people will ever bring them to you. Your workers must go out and get them. Fair enough.

Don't forget your own people. About one-third of the bric-a-brac to be sold will probably come from members of your organization.

A publicity release sent to your local papers and radio station requesting that pieces be donated for your fund-raising effort will yield all the merchandise that can be used for the sale. Have people call a number that will be operative 24 hours a day. How? When no one is on hand to field calls, let your answering machine take the names and numbers of goodwill contributors. Always make things convenient for the public, especially when you are soliciting donations.

There are times when the community goodies might be diminished by other organizations planning to hold a sale about the same time as your own. There is still plenty of saleable junk to be had. Arrange for telephone teams to call the townfolk. You will get all the merchandise you need for the sale from people who only respond when they are solicited.

PICK-UP BRIGADE

Now let's go get 'em. Vehicle power is needed next. Organize pick-up brigades by enlisting people who have station wagons, small trucks, and vans; enlist others who do not mind loading up their cars with household throw-outs. From the master list of contributions, determine what vehicle is needed for each item, the day, and time pick-ups should be made.

Now let's be chauvinistic about this. Gender selection for delicate hauling trips is wise. Women are likely to be more gentle with such items as china, figurines, and crystal.

SALE DAY

Have ample checkout personnel to prevent people from being discouraged by long lines. If the line is moving smoothly with just one person, recycle some of your extra checkout crew to help sell. Keep them on standby, ready to be called back at any time.

On the other hand, if the buying swells to a point that even your enlarged checkout crew can't trim the lines fast enough, think about having one or two people available as "Instant Sales" persons. Wearing a carpenter's apron with pockets to hold change, they can float through the crowds to write up small orders right on the spot.

Muscular helpers will be needed to assist people to carry out sizeable pieces and secure them to customers' cars. Try to get a delivery service to be available to cart big items away for shoppers at a discount fee. They would probably handle several deliveries at one time. Have the names and telephone numbers of local services that customers can call to have the big pieces picked up, if they can't be taken immediately.

APPRAISAL SERVICE

For added revenue, a local professional appraiser might be persuaded to be on hand for the sale days to give people a quick reading on whether or not they have something of special value. Charge three dollars for each piece evaluated. Make it clear that this is a cursory appraisal that will make people aware if they have something utterly worthless or an item that should be evaluated more fully. People are very curious about many of the things they own.

Some appraisers would cooperate as they are the eternal bounty hunters looking for undiscovered treasure. How simple it is to have unsophisticated people bringing them items that might qualify as antique or expensive collectibles. They could bid for these precious pieces right at the sale.

Thrift shop proprietors can also make skillful appraisals. They have enough experience to know the valueless from the potentially valuable.

SALE FREQUENCY

It is best to hold a sale once or twice a year. In this way there is enough time and help to make the events something special. If you establish a good reputation, customers will come back again and again. And through word of mouth, many new ones will be at your future sales as well.

PUBLICITY

Local newspapers and AM-FM radio stations will use publicity announcements of a fund-raising sale. Here is a sample release:

> RUMMAGE SALE
> THORNWOOD-Furniture, clothing, garden tools, books, jewelry, china, and other items will be sold at bargain prices at the annual summer rummage sale of the Community Child Center, 82 Barrow Road, Saturday, July 16 from 9 A.M. to 6 P.M.

Substituting the appropriate information for your organization, use this form to prepare your press release. Send photocopies to all of your local media at least four weeks before the sale.

FIGURE 21. At the Garage Sale Store, silverplate is displayed in these cardboard bins.

FIGURE 22. Bric-a-brac at second hand stores range from old lanterns to china.

FIGURE 23. New merchandise is occasionally found at the Garage Sale Store. A buy-out of sculpture clips and holder sets allowed them to be sold at bargain prices.

FIGURE 24. Special pieces like this primitive clothes washer are among the unusual products found at second-hand shops.

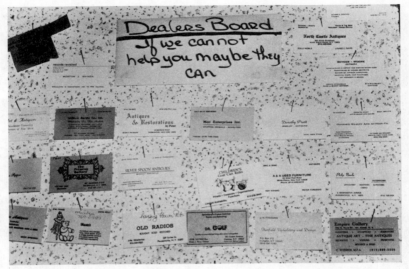

FIGURE 25. The "Dealers Board" at the Garage Sale Store provides a list of places where special services and products can be found.

THRIFT SHOPS

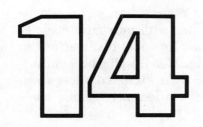

They are called thrift or consignment shops and many use such romantic names as Second Engagement, Deja Vu, The Opportunity Shop, or Antiques & Treasures, but the unglamourous truth is they are all second-hand stores catering to the increasing American demand for used merchandise.

The patrons of these merchants, who sell products with a past, are not all consumers burdened by lean budgets. Many are the same bargain hunters who look for tarnished treasure in the heaping mounds of discards offered at weekend garage sales. Other consumers come to these second-time-around markets hoping to find quality pieces they can restore for their homes.

One executive, whose taste for the best could not be compromised, furnished his new home with purchases made at garage sales and second-hand stores. He could easily afford to buy the best new merchandise available. Despite his comfortable bank account, he was outraged by the inflated prices asked for products that are no match for crafted merchandise made 30 years ago.

A little vision is needed in making the rounds of the thrift and consignment shops. Look beyond the frayed ticking on a smartly designed sofa and visualize it covered with your own choice of new fabric. When you see a scuffed and scratched table, imagine it finished to perfection with the wood tones you like.

Left only to weekends to find quality furniture and other living necessities for your home, it could be a long time before you get everything you want. The thrift and consignment shops have a greater selection of used merchandise and, like other merchants, are open usually six days a week, from 9:00 A.M. to 6:00 P.M.

For people who prefer to get rid of their castoffs with one phone call rather than undertake the rigors of holding a garage sale, no matter how profitable it might be, the second-hand shop is the place to contact. "We buy out everything a person has from antiques to bric-a-brac," said Jill Goldstone of the Garage Sale Store. "You did say you buy everything?" "Yes," said Jill emphatically. "We take it all. We do a complete buyout."

Fingering away a few unruly, long blonde hairs that had fallen over her face, Jill explained, "In this business we risk taking everything a person has to sell. Based on our experience, it pays off. We evaluate the merchandise offered and set a price to buy it all, even when we do not see anything that excites us. We are confident that one or two things we will find in all this junk will cover our acquisition cost. Then anything else we sell is profit."

What happens with things that cannot be sold? Jill has a benevolent way of disposing of her unsaleables. She places them in a free box in front of the store. It is usually filled with toys, bric-a-brac, some china, and such items as a hat box and an old portable typewriter.

"I started this as a community service," Jill noted, "but

I found it had an immediate benefit. Children find toys that interest them and remain outside playing while their mothers are able to browse through my store leisurely. It often makes the difference between a sale and just a quick inspection by a harried mom."

There are regular customers who search for a particular item. They become known as the pot lady, the silverware man, the towel and linen housewife, and the furniture shoppers.

It can all be found at the Garage Sale Store, located in a medium-sized warehouse. The front portion has been converted into an attractive shop with shelves holding items that sell from a dollar to $25, paintings that are priced up to several hundred dollars, furniture, and every type of small household product. Neatly stacked in a rack with drawers is flatware—spoons, forks, knives—all selling for ten cents.

Can you bargain? Not for anything costing less than five dollars. Negotiation is expected for everything else. It is the built-in tradition of second-hand shop patrons.

The back room contains most of the large pieces of furniture. It is so packed that some of the most dramatically styled chairs are suspended from rafters by heavy rope. While this creates a startling display, at first glance the gutted seats with springs punched through the bottom might make the casual customer wonder why they are there. A closer inspection reveals detailed and artistic woodwork that makes refinishing these unique pieces worth the cost and effort. It takes the kind of imagination the executive had when redoing his new home from purchases made at thrift and consignment shops.

Jill nodded affirmatively and said, "When that piece is redone, it will eventually command a price much higher than the cost of the purchase and the refinishing."

Acquiring some of the better buys offered by the Garage Sale Shop is the mission of special teams organized by husband Mitch Goldstone. He has housewives, police, firemen, and telephone company employees assigned to covering as many garage sales during the weekend as possible and buying items that are being sold at giveaway prices. Briefed on what is needed for the Garage Sale Store, they come back in a very short time with excellent products that are high revenue pieces.

The second-hand store is where you can shop for a bargain or quickly dispose of anything you want to sell.

ADVERTISING AND PROMOTION

Now, how do you attract customers to your sale? Through advertising and sales promotion suitable for this personal venture. The techniques that attract buyers to your home are relatively simple. Study the advertising and promotional suggestions made and use the ones that are right for your type of sale.

While the big advertising agencies have specialists who analyze publications to determine which ones reach the special markets needed for their clients, your choices will be very limited. This is truly a blessing, as it will cost you comparatively little to alert garage sale addicts to your special event.

MEDIA SELECTION

If you have one in your community, the most effective publication for advertising homestyle sales is in the Pennysaver. It is an 8- by 11-inch newspaper devoted entirely to display and classified ads. Found on nearly every page of the publication are ads for garage, yard, moving, estate, multifamily, and home contents sales. In fact, in one July issue there were over 100 such appeals to shoppers.

Almost every area in the country is served by a weekly paper, and many are covered by small dailies that publish mainly town and community news. Too competitive? Not necessarily. Yard sale buffs go to the sales nearest their homes. Other shoppers look for different types of sales and search for special merchandise. You might have just what 60 or 70 people want.

What you have working for you is

Merchandise
Type of sale
Geographical convenience

Acknowledging the garage sale boom in the nation, local dailies and weekly papers now have classified columns for garage sale listings. The Patent Trader in Mount Kisco, New York, encourages readers to advertise in this section through its own advertising in the paper. The classified section in your local weekly probably has a similar section for yard sales.

If you are not aware of any weekly paper in your area, check the listing for these papers in the *Editor & Publisher Yearbook*, a publication you generally find in the central library of your town. You can also call the media department of an advertising agency and ask what paper you should use. People in this profession are extremely gracious.

Of course, if you know anyone who has held a garage sale, ask them where they advertised. You will also get some helpful advice by calling the proprietor of a thrift shop. These merchants follow the ads for private sales as they are interested in buying out the leftovers.

WRITING THE AD

Here are some questions frequently asked by people faced with writing ad copy for the first time:

How Can I Make My Ad Exciting?

Follow agency pros and start your advertisement with a high-powered adjective.

> Giant Garage Sale
> Super Tag Sale
> Gigantic Yard Sale
> Enormous Driveway Sale
> Monster Multifamily Sale
> Tremendous Moving Sale

While this kind of hype will bring more customers, the most effective appeal to prospective patrons is in the merchandise you list.

How Do I Decide What Is Special?

List items being offered that are appropriate to the season: chain saw, lawnmower, weed cutter, snow plow, snow tires. Antiques, collectibles, and furniture always pull well.

Should I List Prices?

Only for large items that are obvious bargains. Since the condition of merchandise is such an important factor in determining the purchase price, just list specific items and general categories such as baby clothes, toys, and garden tools.

Should I List
My Telephone Number?

It is advisable not to as you will receive many calls from people who want to inspect your wares in advance and from others who will give you excuses as to why they must come to your sale an hour or two before it opens. However, should you live in such a remote area that finding your house would be difficult, it would be wise to put your phone number in and have people call for directions.

How Do I Handle
Directions in the Copy?

List an exit off a main highway or road that is near your house, then specify if motorists should make a left or right turn. At the very next intersection, you should have the first sign directing people to your sale.

How Should I Place My Signs?

Carol Kiley advises that, from the main road, you put a sign at the end of each block or at the next turn in the road. After two or three signs noting the garage sale, date, and address, you can use signs that only have a large arrow on them. This is a very effective way to keep the traffic flowing to your house. Don't forget to have a big "Tag Sale" sign in front of your home.

When Should I Put My Ad In?

About three days before your sale. Of course, this will depend upon when your local paper comes out. The Yorktown Heights, New York, Pennysaver comes out on Tuesday. However, people using a daily paper can place the ad in the Wednesday edition.

Usually a daily will give you a discount price for a three-day insertion. Take it.

Should My Ad List Alternate Dates in Case of Rain?

Yes. Unless you decide to hold the sale rain or shine, put a rain date in your ad postponing the sale to the following week. Good weather is definitely an asset. However, for a home contents sale it does not matter, as people will be inside.

SOME SAMPLE ADS

The following ads illustrate the points covered in this chapter:

MONSTER MULTIFAMILY SALE, July 16-17, 10-6. Air conditioner, lawnmower, seed spreader, queen-sized bed, desk, typewriter, and bric-a-brac. Crowe Hill Road, Hartsdale.

GIANT GARAGE SALE, May 3-4, 9-5. Electric grill, guitar, fish tanks, appliances, china, and many more bargains. Hollow Brook Road, Peekskill, just off the Taconic Parkway.

HUGE TAG SALE, Nov. 10-11, 10-4. Craftsman snow blower $95; G78-14 studded snow tires, glass belted $50; skis $40; freezer $25; garden tools; lamps; appliances and lots more. Exit 5 on Route 684, turn left and follow signs.

SUPER YARD SALE, June 8-9, 10-4, Park Terrace, Croton. Antique lamps, oil paintings, lighting fixtures, collectible dolls, posters, toys, and bric-a-brac. Rain date June 15-16.

MAMMOTH MOVING SALE, August 17-18, 8-3. Over 20 years accumulation. Furniture, sterling, flatware, oriental rugs, bookcases, pool table, stereo, antiques, electric trains, desks, spinet piano, almost anything you need. Cash only.

SIGNS AND FLYERS

Susan Posmentier, who is a commercial artist, strongly recommends using black letters four to six inches high, placed on light colored paper. She said that this sign can be read from a distance of 25 feet.

Susan frowns upon using any kind of design. "It only interferes with the message." She also recommends that signs be kept at eye level, which simply means not too high. A staple gun should be used to tack them to trees and poles.

Investigate the possibility of buying preprinted garage sale signs. These colorful pieces have the words GARAGE SALE in capital letters on the top, a white space in the center for you to write in the dates and address, and a large arrow below. They are attractive and very easy to read. Put the signs up the morning of the sale.

Put your yard sale information on index cards and place them on bulletin boards at supermarkets, nursery schools, laundromats, beauty parlors, your church or temple, or any clubs you belong to. If someone in your family commutes, leave signs in the car window while the car is parked at the station.

Alert your neighbors by sending them an announcement in the form of a letter. If you have artistic ability, you can make a colorful flyer. This is the place for art work. You also can use this piece of handiwork for the various community bulletin boards.

FIGURE 26. This preprinted garage sale sign can be purchased at most hardware stores. Insert your address and dates of your sale in the blank white space. This sign is attached to an outside wall of the Garage Sale Store.

FLEA MARKET OUTLET

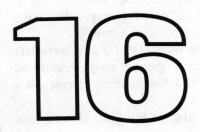

If you have a special, entrepreneurial spirit or want to avoid the crush of people coming to your home and trampling all over your lawn and driveway, you can take your merchandise to where the buyers are: the flea market.

Art and Dot Olson, who are now regular weekend flea market vendors, began by holding occasional yard sales. When forced to sell their leftovers at a fraction of their value to dealers, thrift, and consignment shops, Dotty decided to experiment. They rented space at a small, local flea market and discovered that they sold out everything they had.

"All we needed then was a table and two chairs for us to sit on and wait for customers," reflected Dotty. "We were astonished at the number of people who were there."

When they got rid of their own castoffs and were left with a clean basement and an empty garage, they considered acquiring merchandise and doing the flea market circuit on a regular basis.

Art Olson noted, "I was always working at odd jobs

during weekends to earn extra money we needed. At the flea markets, we found that we were making so much more money that it was worth the time we both invested in it."

The Olsons, who have expanded to four tables, a station wagon, and a van, now sell mostly new merchandise. Flea markets, which once were mainly huge garage sales where junk prevailed over antiques and collectibles, are today an interesting balance between the new and the old.

According to Dotty Olson, retailers have discovered that flea markets are an excellent outlet for unloading excessive inventory at reduced prices. At a mammoth flea market held at an airport at Stormville, New York, there were over 600 vendors selling their wares. New products were in ample supply: radios, clocks, clothes (designer labels), brand name men's underwear, umbrellas, kerosene heaters, and all kinds of household items.

FLEA MARKET BOOM

With the growth of flea markets throughout the country, these merchandise marts attract such a huge volume of traffic today that they are being held at race tracks, athletic fields, parking lots, in the street, or at urban centers. On Sundays the lower Broadway section of New York City is clogged for blocks with amateur vendors. Many people just drive down, find a corner or other available space, and spread out their wares on the street. They then sit back and wait for customers who come faithfully, rain or shine, although vendors expect fewer patrons when it rains.

Outdoor markets operate every Sunday until late November, when the winter winds chill both the customers and the vendors away. Waiting for patrons from 10:00 A.M. until dusk during the heat and rain is exhausting enough. When the crackling cold sets in, it's time to take a hiatus until spring.

However, flea markets operate year-round. When the winter comes, the Olsons don't hibernate but get space at the giant indoor facilities usually set up in unused warehouses. Space here is in demand by permanent vendors like the Olsons and one space can cost $50. Owners of these climate-controlled centers often provide entertainment and have food for sale as customer incentives.

The Olsons advise that people who become flea market peddlers only when it is time to clear the house of discards do their selling at a community venture. Schools, churches, temples, and other organizations arrange flea markets as a fundraising enterprise. Space costs from five to ten dollars and the entire event is usually promoted as a local festival.

FLEA MARKET SHOPPING

The popularity of flea markets is international. One of the biggest in the world is held in London every Saturday. Offerings range from the usual bric-a-brac to expensive antiques and collectibles. Many sharp-eyed buyers have made windfall purchases in this British market. Not luck. They knew when a priceless piece had escaped the notice of the vendor and was selling for a fraction of its value.

The wily buyers who prowl these markets, searching for overlooked treasure, seem to agree that it is more fun than playing the stock market and certainly much less risky.

Good hunting.

LOCAL LAWS

17

In most of the country it is still unnecessary to get any permit to hold your garage sale. However, with the number of these sales soaring each year, a few municipalities have introduced mild legal controls. It is advisable to call your local police department and inquire if a permit is needed in your area.

Some people, dazzled with the profits that can be made from these junk sales, were holding them every week, essentially running a flea market in their yards and driveways. In many cases signs were placed at the curb nearest these home-sale proprietors advertising items that people could come in and buy at anytime. The City Council of New Rochelle, New York, responding to the pleas of disturbed residents to curb this practice, passed local laws regulating garage sales.

The first version of New Rochelle's law actually stipulated that permits would be necessary in order to conduct such a sale. However, protests from citizens that the law was excessive prompted the town council to modify its legal requirements. The law that was passed prohibits any household from having more than three sales a year.

The ordinance also mandates that everything sold must be owned by the seller or his or her family. Sales must be conducted in a garage, carport, or rear yard only, and for just three consecutive days or two consecutive weekends.

With the penalty for violators only a ten dollar fine, some homeowners, eager to maintain the profitable yield from their weekend merchandise marathons, might consider this a small price to pay for breaking the law. For your sale, play it safe and see if there are any legal limits to what you can do.

INDEX